Theme Centers for Dramatic Play

Authors	Judie Bertolino
	Linda Milliken
	Kathy Rogers
Editor	Kathy Rogers
Cover Design	Mary Jo Keller
Page Design	Kathy Rogers
Illustrations	Mary Jo Keller

©1996 Edupress • P.O. Box 883 • Dana Point, CA 92629
EP106   ISBN 1-56472-106-X

TABLE OF CONTENTS

TABLE OF CONTENTS

INTRODUCTION

Each center presented in this book is based on five common furnishings: kitchen unit, bookshelf, tables, chairs, costume box. You probably already have these furnishings plus the materials you need to get started. How much you add is up to you and the amount of space you have available in your classroom. You do not have to make every prop or provide every activity in order for your children to have a productive experience in the centers.

Begin by designating a space for your ongoing dramatic play center. Arrange the kitchen unit, book shelf, and at least one table in the space. Look for these features in the book for help:

CENTER SET UP
- **Floorplan.** Rearrange furnishings to fit available space.
- **Furnishings and Accessories.** Look here for a complete list of all center materials and their placement within the center. Each basic furnishing may be given a different name in order to spark children's interest; the kitchen unit may be called the ship's galley, but it is still the standard kitchen unit stocked with basics like play food, dishes, and dishpans. The art table should include scissors, glue, paper, and other art materials. Add other materials as suggested.
- **Bare-Budget Furnishings.** Here you'll find suggestions for creating low-cost furnishings for each center.
- **Center Enhancements.** Decorate the center with simple accessories in order to add visual appeal to stimulate childrens' interest, using things that are easy to find or easily made.

PROPS TO MAKE
Each prop serves as the basis for a developmental activity to set up in the center. They are all made using recycled or easy-to-obtain materials.

TEACHING TIPS
- **Center Tips.** Here are suggested ways to introduce a new center theme to your students. Review the safety tips together.
- **Center Variations.** Younger learners need frequent environmental changes. Here are some ideas for simple additions that bring a new focus to the current center.

DEVELOPMENTAL ACTIVITIES
Open-ended activities allow children to explore and create at their own learning level.

RESOURCES AND MORE
Teacher-directed activities extend the center theme. Follow the suggestions for integrating community resources both inside and outside the classroom.

LITERATURE LIST
Stock the bookshelf with related books for children to browse through. Spark discussion and interest during circle time. Send a list home to parents .

PARENT LETTER
Get help! Reproduce the letter to send home well in advance of each scheduled center. Invite parents to help build, set up, and provide the materials you will be using.

CHECKLISTS AND MORE
- **Page 301.** Many props can be used in more than one center. This quick-reference prop list will provide the spark for cross-over use!
- **Page 302.** Time management and student evaluation tips.
- **Page 303.** Observation log for use as an indivualized tool fo evaluate student development.

Theme Centers for Dramatic Play

Chuck's Diner

CENTER SET-UP

FLOORPLAN

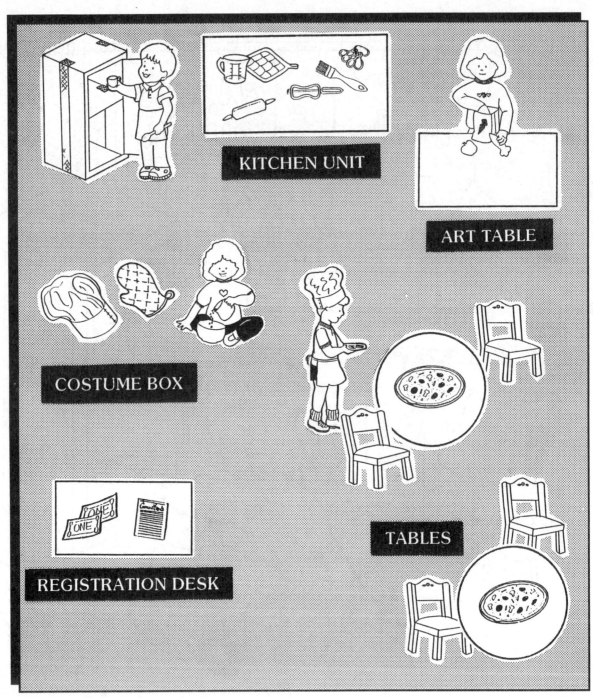

KITCHEN UNIT

ART TABLE

COSTUME BOX

TABLES

REGISTRATION DESK

CENTER SET-UP

FURNISHINGS AND ACCESSORIES

Miscellaneous
- Play money
- Receipt books
- Serving trays

Registration Desk
- Menus (Props to Make)
- Telephone
- Clipboard & pen
- Telephone book

Clothes Rack (page 206)

Refrigerator (Bare-Budget Furnishings)
- Play food
- Ice cube trays
- Refrigerator food containers

Art Table
- Food shape sponges
- Doggie bags (Props to Make)
- Magazine pictures of food (Activity page—Food Sort)
- Paper plates

Costume Box
- Aprons (Props to Make)
- Suit coats
- Various jewelry
- Chef's hats (Props to Make)
- Ties
- Hats
- Cooking mitts
- Purses
- Dresses

Kitchen Unit
- Dishes
- Dish towels
- Pots & pans
- Silverware
- Dishwashing set-up
- Cookbooks
- Measuring cups
- Measuring spoons
- Uncooked rice in containers (Activity page—Measure Food)
- Food scale (Activity page—Food Scale)

Tables
- Place mats or tablecloths
- Vases & silk flowers

9

Center Set-Up

Bare-Budget Furnishings

Refrigerator
Materials
- Large cardboard box
- Medium cardboard box
- Scissors
- Masking tape

Directions
1. Select two rectangular boxes so that the smaller box fits inside the larger box.
2. Seal all flaps on the large box with tape.
3. Cut the side of the large box to make a door.
4. Cut flaps away from the top of the smaller box.
5. Place the smaller box inside the larger box, open side facing front.

10

CENTER ENHANCEMENTS

City Skyline

On a piece of butcher paper, sponge-paint a city skyline to use outside (behind) your restaurant sign.

Window

Create a window out of yardsticks painted and stapled to the wall, or use butcher paper and tempera paint to create a window.

Cafe Curtains

Use a fabric remnant stapled to the wall in gathers to replicate a cafe curtain. Matching dish towels may be used, also.

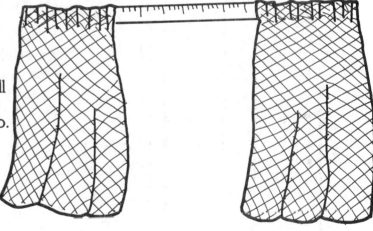

Restaurant Sign

On a piece of butcher paper, paint the name of the restaurant in tempera paint. Attach to the wall.

 PROPS TO MAKE

 MENUS

(Prop is appropriate for child participation)
Materials
- Tagboard
- Magazines
- Glue sticks
- Scissors
- Markers

Directions
1. Cut tagboard to desired shape.
2. Attach food pictures to poster board using glue sticks.
3. Use markers to add the words describing the food and the cost of each item.

APRON

(Prop is appropriate for child participation)
Materials
- Plain white muslin
- Yarn (pre-cut to desired length)
- Fabric markers or regular markers
- Tape
- Scissors
- Hole punch

Directions
1. Tape ends of yarn.
2. Punch holes in fabric.
3. Thread yarn through holes.
4. Decorate fabric with markers.

12

PROPS TO MAKE

CHEF'S HAT

Materials
- White tagboard
- White tissue paper
- Cellophane tape
- Stapler

Directions
1. Cut a strip of tagboard to fit around a child's head.
2. Staple the two ends of the tagboard together.
3. Use tape to fasten the ends of the tissue paper to the inside of the tagboard, shaping to fit over head.

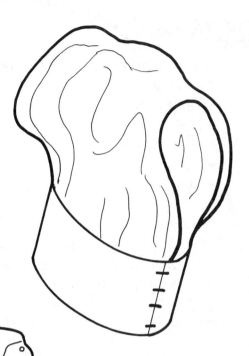

DOGGIE BAGS

(Prop is appropriate for child participation)

Materials
- Plain white paper bags
- Sponges cut in food shapes (patterns following)
- Tempera paint
- Pie pans

Directions
1. Mix paint in pie pans.
2. Set out bags, paint and sponges.
3. Invite children to decorate bags. (Make some for school and some to go home.)

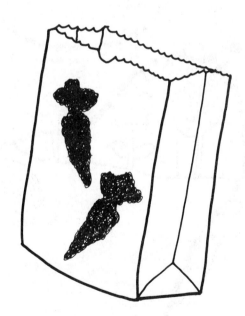

13

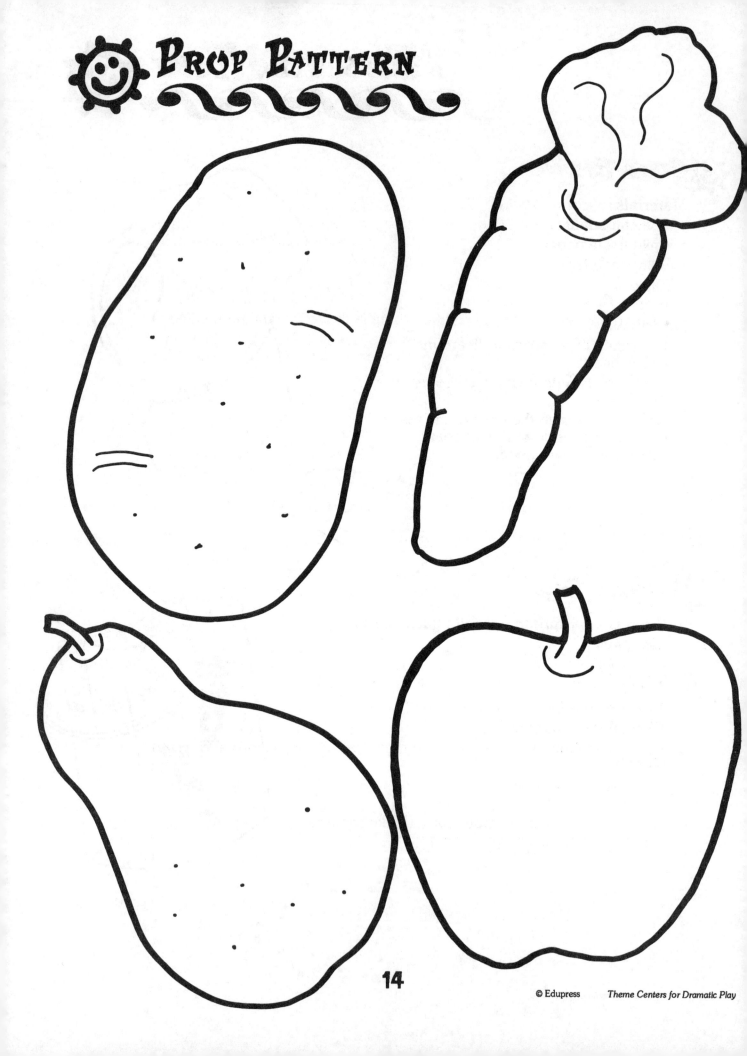

PROP PATTERN

© Edupress   *Theme Centers for Dramatic Play*

☼ CENTER TIPS

Introducing the Center
During circle time, talk about the children's experiences at a restaurant. Ask open-ended questions: What is your favorite restaurant? What do you like to order? Who goes to the restaurant with you?

Safety Tips
• Determine the number of children to be in the restaurant at one time.
• Let children suggest ways to decide who is next to be in the restaurant. (Children could sign up to play in the center at the registration desk.)
• Caution children that the rice is uncooked and not for eating.

☼ CENTER VARIATIONS

Pizza Restaurant
• Make pizzas from cardboard circles, decorated with red glue for sauce, sawdust for cheese, and paper circles for pepperoni.
• Set tables with red-checked tablecloths and candles.
• Display travel posters about Italy.

Fast Food
• Provide foam food containers.
• Post menu board on wall.
• Purchase party favor toys for "kid meal" prizes (be cautious about size).

Ice Cream Parlor
• Cover oatmeal cartons and decorate as ice cream containers.
• Provide ice cream scoops, play dough for ice cream, and paper cones.
• Post ice cream menu on the wall.

Developmental Activities

☼ Measure Food

Measure rice into containers using measuring cups and measuring spoons.

Skills To Build
• Acquiring skills with tools and equipment
• Manipulating materials
• Discovering relations through direct experience

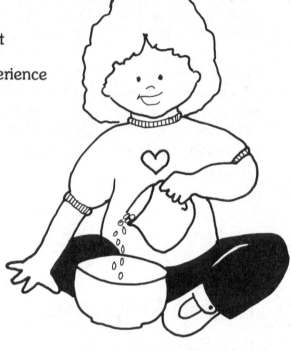

☼ Food Sort

Use food patterns (page 14) to cut shapes from construction paper. Sort into Doggie Bags (Props to Make). Let children determine criteria.

Skills To Build
• Arranging a set of objects

DEVELOPMENTAL ACTIVITIES

ORDER UP

Role-play being restaurant waiters and take food orders from customers. Create meals by selecting magazine pictures of food items and gluing them to a paper plate.

Skills To Build
• Listening
• Nutrition awareness

FOOD SCALE

Use a food scale to measure and compare the weight of a single piece of one food to another.

Skills To Build
• Seriation—comparing attributes (bigger/smaller, heavier/lighter)
• Arranging items in order from largest to smallest

17

☼ Literature List

☼ Picture Books

• Marge's Diner
by Gail Gibbons;
Harper LB 1989. (PS-2)
A picture book that explains the
workings of a diner.

• A Chef
by Douglas Florian;
Greenwillow LB 1992. (PS-2)
The hustle and bustle of a
professional kitchen during a chef's
workday are described.

• First Look at Growing Food
by Clair Llewellyn;
Stevens LB 1991. (1-2)
Easy-to-read text and bright color
photos tell about how food gets to
the eater.

• What's on My Plate
by Ruth Belov Gross;
Macmillan 1990. (PS-1)
These simple direct answers about
food are tuned to a child's frame of
reference.

• Make Me a Peanut Butter
Sandwich (and a Glass of Milk)
by Ken Robbins;
Scholastic 1992. (PS-3)
Photos and text tell how a favorite
snack for children gets to the table.

• Let's Eat!
by True Kelley;
Dutton 1989. (K-2)
A look at where food comes from
and how people eat it.

☼ Books to Read Aloud

• Marcel the Pastry Chef
by Marianna Mayer;
Bantam 1991. (PS-1)
A dish-washing hippo longs to
become a pastry chef.

• What's It Like to Be a Chef?
by Susan K Poskanzer;
Troll LB 1990. (K-3)
Betsy finds out what her uncle, a
chef, does in a behind-the-scenes
look at a restaurant.

• Potluck
by Anne Shelby;
Orchard LB 1991. (PS-2)
Young guests at a dinner party bring
foods that begin with the same letter
as their name.

• Breakfast by Molly
by Ruth Radlauer;
Simon & Schuster 1991. (PS-K)
Molly makes breakfast for mother—
a peanut-butter sandwich and
chocolate sauce on cereal.

• Potluck
by Tobi Tobias;
Lothrop LB 1993. (K-3)
When grandmother says it's "pot
luck" for dinner, it really means a
day of cooking and preparation.

• Cloudy With a Chance of
Meatballs
by Judith Barrett;
Macmillan 1978. (K-3)
In the land of Chew and Swallow,
food falls from the skies.

18

RESOURCES & RELATED ACTIVITIES

- Find food posters from various restaurants (ask restaurant managers).

- Invite restaurant owner or waitress to visit.

- Do kitchen-gadget painting. Dip gadgets into tempera paint and press on paper.

- Invite chef/cook to visit.

- Visit a fast food restaurant for a tour.

- Visit a pizza parlor for a tour.

- Visit an ice cream parlor for a tour.

- Make pizza in class for snack. Have two children work on one pizza.

- Go to a restaurant supply store and buy some utensils for the housekeeping area.

- Go to the grocery store and buy the ingredients to make a simple recipe.

- Have a parent visit the class and cook a simple recipe.

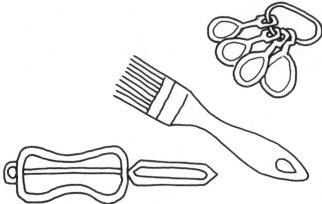

- Cut vegetables in half through the center. Dip into prepared tempera paint in pie pans. Press onto paper.

- Put samples of foods with a variety of flavors in dishes to taste. Make a "blindfold" by covering the lenses of sunglasses with black paper. Foods to try: oranges, marshmallow, popcorn, raisins, pretzels, round oat cereal, carrots, celery, bananas.

- Make a large food collage by cutting out pictures of food and gluing on a large piece of butcher paper.

19

Dear Parents:

We are preparing a Chuck's Diner Theme Center in our classroom during these dates: _____. This center will provide an opportunity for the children to participate in dramatic play and will serve as a basis for classroom discussion and learning activities. Below you will find a list of items that we need to furnish the center:

☐ Muslin fabric

☐ Table cloth

☐ Tissue paper

☐ Food scale

☐ Play Money

☐ Paper place mats

☐ Vase with silk flowers

☐ Plain white paper bags

☐ Pie pans

☐ _____

Please return the items checked above by _____.

You can support the use of this center by talking to your child about the theme, planning family excursions related to the theme, or by sharing books that will provide your child with more information. A suggested literature list is available upon request.

Parent Name _____

Phone Number _____   ☐ I would love to help!

COUNTRY LANE GENERAL STORE

Center Set-Up

Floorplan

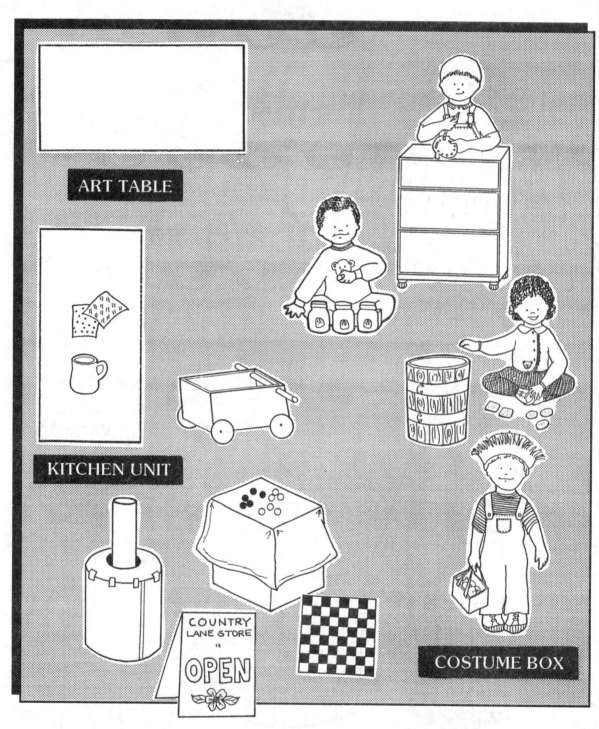

ART TABLE

KITCHEN UNIT

COUNTRY LANE STORE IS OPEN

COSTUME BOX

22

Theme Centers for Dramatic Play

CENTER SET-UP

☼ FURNISHINGS AND ACCESSORIES

Miscellaneous
- Shopping Cart (Bare-Budget Furnishings)
- Pot-Belly Stove (Bare-Budget Furnishings)
- Checker Board & Checkers (Props to Make)

Art Table
- Play dough
- Play dough tools
- Brushes
- Kitchen gadgets
- Hole punches
- Pads & pencils

Costume Box
- Shirts
- Jackets
- Skirts
- Belts
- Aprons
- Shoes
- Hats
- Purses
- Tote bags

Kitchen Unit
- Soap, lotion, brushes
- Coffee mugs
- Assorted plastic food
- Assorted food packages
- Sewing supplies: darning needles, thread, buttons, measuring tape

Drying Rack
- Dish towels & dish cloths
- Place mats
- Fabric pieces

Bookcase
- Magazines
- Paperback books
- Playing cards, games & puzzles
- Lacing Cards (Props to Make) and yarn stored in a basket
- Candy Jars & Gumdrops (Props to Make)

23

☼ BARE-BUDGET FURNISHINGS

Shopping Cart
Materials
• Large cardboard box
• Two dowels, 1/2 x 28 inches (1.27 x 67 cm)
• One dowel, 1 x 36 inches (2.54 cm x 1 m)
• 4 large coffee can lids
• 4 nails   • Knife
• Hammer

Directions
1. Cut four holes in the base of box. Cut two holes in top of box.
2. Slide shorter dowels through lower holes. Nail coffee can lids to ends of dowels to form wheels.
3. Slide longer dowel through upper holes to form handles.

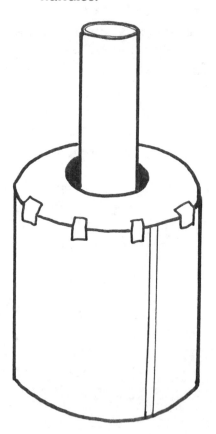

Pot-Belly Stove
Materials
• 2 pieces black tagboard
• Masking tape   • Scissors

Directions
1. Form a cylinder with one piece of tagboard, taping to secure.
2. Make stove top by cutting a 12-inch (30 cm) circle of tagboard.
3. Cut 4-inch (10 cm) hole in center of top for stove pipe. Tape stove top to cylinder as shown.
4. Create stove pipe by cutting tagboard piece 4 inches x 2 feet (10 x 61 cm).
5. Form into a cylinder and fit into top hole.

CENTER ENHANCEMENTS

Sandwich Board

Tape two sections of cardboard (2 x 2 feet/ 61 x 61 cm) together at the top with duct tape. Stand at entrance to General Store and use to display signs.

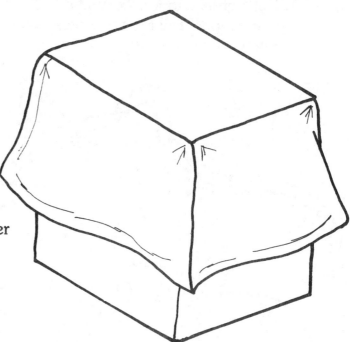

Checkerboard Game Table

Invert a cardboard box. Cover with butcher paper, an old towel or a piece of fabric.

Cracker Barrel

Cover a wastebasket with brown butcher paper. Decorate with markers or paint to simulate a barrel.

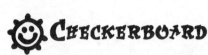 Props to Make

☀ Checkerboard

Materials
- Tagboard
- Tempera paint
- Scissors
- Ruler
- Brushes

Directions
1. Cut tagboard to form a square.
2. Use tempera paint to paint alternating squares on the board.

☀ Lacing Cards

Materials
- Tagboard (red, orange, yellow)
- Scissors
- Hole punch
- Yarn
- Masking tape

Directions
1. Draw orange, apple and banana shapes on tagboard and cut out.
2. Punch holes around the edge of each card, spacing 1 inch (2.54 cm) apart.
3. Cut 1 yard (1 m) of yarn per card. Wrap tape around the ends of the yarn.
4. Put cards and yarn in a basket so that children have easy access to them.

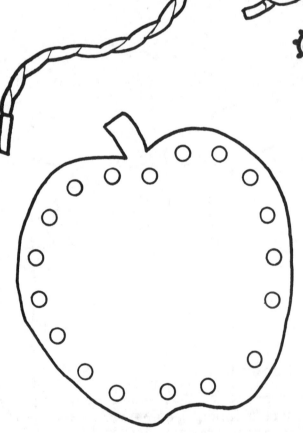

26

Props to Make

☺ Cracker Barrel Crackers

Materials
- Cardboard
- Scissors
- White puffy paint

Directions
1. Cut a variety of cracker shapes from brown cardboard.
2. Use white puffy paint to make dots that suggest salt grains.

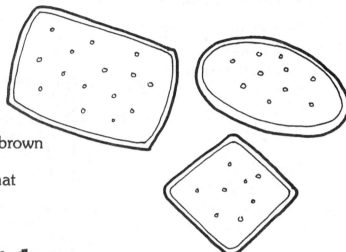

☺ Checkers

Materials
- Soda bottle lids
- Stickers (plain/single color)

Directions
Put stickers on half the soda lids only, to differentiate between two sets of men.

☺ Gum Drop Jars

Materials
- Patterns, following page
- Construction paper in a variety of colors
- 4 small milk cartons
- Scissors
- Glue
- Crayons

Directions
1. Reproduce pattern page twice.
2. Wash and dry milk cartons. Cut off tops.
3. Color the gum drops: 6 each of 4 different colors.
4. Cut and glue a jar to the front of each milk carton.
5. Glue a different color gum drop to each jar.

27

PROP PATTERN

28

Theme Centers for Dramatic Play

TEACHING TIPS

☼ CENTER TIPS

Introducing the Center
Come to class with a basket full of real produce and canned goods. Ask children to identify the items and ask about their experiences at a grocery store.

Safety Tips
• At school, scissors are for cutting paper and fabric only.
• Small items (buttons, etc.) do not go in the mouth.
• The "sandwich board" cannot be worn or used as a tent.

☼ CENTER VARIATIONS

Produce Store
Add baskets and small cardboard boxes. Place real or plastic fruit or vegetables in baskets.

Discount Store
Add small appliances, toys, and sports equipment. Display newspaper "special" flyers. Place all items in store in boxes, bins, or laundry baskets. Label each basket with a single price sign and provide play coins.

# DEVELOPMENTAL ACTIVITIES

☺ CRACKER COUNT

Place crackers (Props to Make) in the cracker barrel for sorting and counting.

Skills To Build
- Shape recognition
- Shape names
- Size comparison
- Sorting
- Counting

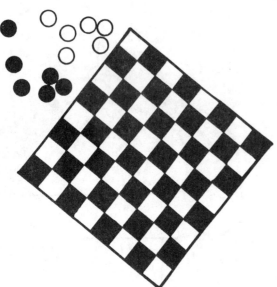

☺ CHECKER CHALLENGE/ DOMINO DILEMMA

Put out boxes containing checkers and dominoes. Model playing the games **or** "block-build" with them.

Skills To Build
- Small motor
- Visual discrimination
- Critical thinking

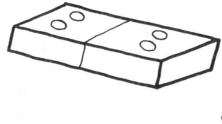

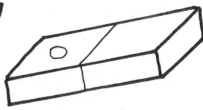

30

Theme Centers for Dramatic Play

DEVELOPMENTAL ACTIVITIES

☼ FRUIT LACING

Place lacing cards and yarn in a basket in the art center, available for children to discover and use.

Skills To Build
• Small motor skills
• Concept of in and out
• Shape

☼ GUM DROP SORTING

Sort and count gum drops into jars by color.

Skills To Build
• Color recognition
• Sorting
• Counting

LITERATURE LIST

PICTURE BOOKS

• *Tom and Pippo Go Shopping*
by Helen Oxenbury;
Macmillan 1989. (PS)
A toddler and his monkey on a
shopping adventure.

• *Mom's Home*
by Jan Ormerod;
Lothrop 1987. (PS)
Sorting through mom's shopping
basket is an adventure for a cat and
a young boy.

• *Mama, Papa and Baby Joe*
by Niki Daly;
Viking 1991. (PS-K)
A most unusual family goes out on a
very weird shopping trip.

• *Lily and the Present*
by Christine Ross;
Houghton 1992 (PS-2)
Lily goes shopping for a present for
her new baby brother.

• *Eating the Alphabet; Fruits and
   Vegetables from A to Z*
by Lois Elert;
Harcourt 1989. (PS-1)
An eye-catching alphabet book.

• *Would You Rather...*
by John Burningham.
Harper LB 1978. (PS-2)
Riding a bull into the supermarket is
one of the imaginative situations
described in this humorous book.

BOOKS TO READ ALOUD

• *The Witches Supermarket*
by Susan Meddaugh;
Houghton LB 1991. (PS-3)
On Halloween, Helen finds herself
in a strange supermarket selling
goodies like scum milk.

• *General Store*
by Rachel Field;
Greenwillow LB 1988. (PS-1)
A poem that extols the charms of
the old fashioned store.

• *The Storekeeper*
by Tracy Campbell Pearson;
Puffin paper 1991. (PS-2)
The general store in the story is on
the green of a New England Village.

• *We Keep a Store*
by Anne Shelby
Orchard LB 1990. (K-2)
A young girl tells about the country
store that her family operates.

• *Don't Forget the Bacon!*
by Pat Hutchins;
Greenwillow LB 1976. (K-3)
A young boy mixes up the shopping
list on a trip to the grocery store.

• *The Potato Man*
by Megan McDonald;
Walker LB 1991. (K-3)
Grampa recalls the time when his
neighborhood was regularly visited
by peddlers.

Theme Centers for Dramatic Play

RESOURCES & MORE

RESOURCES & RELATED ACTIVITIES

- Make a shopping list in class.

- Take the list and visit a store to buy the items.

- Collect labels from food packages and coupons. Create a collage with them.

- Create a display of stacked bar soap that might be found in a general store. Measure the stack. Try a different arrangement.

- Using a simple sewing pattern, stitch it to fabric and invite the children to try cutting it out.

- With teacher, kids and parent helpers learn to sew a button on fabric using large darning needles.

- Using Joy™ or Dawn™ liquid soap, make bubbles and use them outside.

- Using small bars of Ivory™ soap and heavy plastic knives, try soap carving.

- Make potpourri to sell in the store, then give it as a gift.

- Snack on crackers and compare and name the different shapes.

- Make a magazine collage of things you would find in a general store.

- Create bins of bulk dry goods such as rice or beans and practice small motor skills by scooping the items into paper bags.

Edupress   *Theme Centers for Dramatic Play*

Dear Parents:

We are preparing a Country Lane General Store Theme Center in our classroom during these dates: _____. This center will provide an opportunity for the children to participate in dramatic play and will serve as a basis for classroom discussion and learning activities. Below you will find a list of items that we need to furnish the center:

☐ Sewing patterns   ☐ Empty food containers

☐ Kitchen gadgets   ☐ Joy™ or Dawn™ dishwashing liquid

☐ Magazines   ☐ Bottle caps

☐ Buttons   ☐ Ivory™ soap

☐ Fabric   ☐ _____

Please return the items checked above by _____.

You can support the use of this center by talking to your child about the theme, planning family excursions related to the theme, or by sharing books that will provide your child with more information. A suggested literature list is available upon request.

Parent Name _____

Phone Number _____ ☐ I would love to help!

34

Sweet Stuff Bakery

Edupress   *Theme Centers for Dramatic Play*

CENTER SET-UP

FLOORPLAN

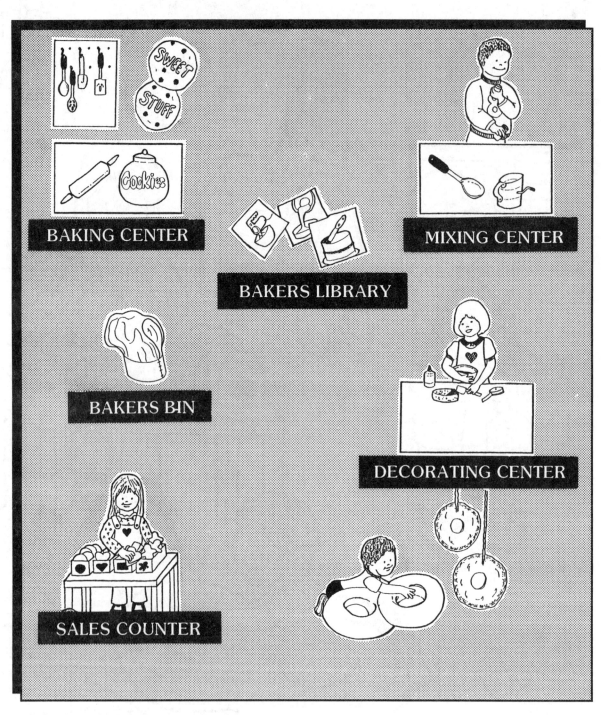

BAKING CENTER

BAKERS LIBRARY

MIXING CENTER

BAKERS BIN

DECORATING CENTER

SALES COUNTER

Theme Centers for Dramatic Play

CENTER SET-UP

FURNISHINGS AND ACCESSORIES

Sales Counter
- Paper Bags
- Tongs
- Shoe box display (Center Enhancements)
- Cookie jars
- Cupcakes (Props to Make)
- Play bakery items
- Cash register
- Play money
- Display case
- Bakery

Baking Center
- Cookie sheets
- Muffin tins
- Muffin cups
- Cake pans
- Pie pans
- Play dough
- Rolling pin
- Cookie cutters
- Plastic eggs
- Waxed paper

Bakers Bin
- Aprons
- Hair nets
- Chef's hat
- White shirts
- Purses
- Wallets

Bakers Library
- Donut cushions (inflated pool inner tubes)
- Bookcase
- Cookbooks with recipes for pastries, cakes & cookies
- Pastry Pictures (Props to Make)

Mixing Center
- Bowls
- Spoons
- Spatulas
- Sifter
- Spice Sniffers (Props to Make)
- Hand beater
- Measuring cups
- Food coloring
- Flour
- Plastic spray bottles filled with water

Decorating Center
- Muffin cups
- Glue
- Decorating sprinkles
- Plastic knives
- Cardboard cookies (Props to Make)
- Cake pattern
- Art supplies
- Layer cakes (Props to Make)
- Canned frosting

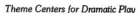

37

Center Set-Up

Bare-Budget Furnishings

Display Case
Materials
- 6 to 8 shoe boxes
- Double-sided tape
- Spray paint

Directions
1. Use double-sided tape to connect shoe boxes side-by-side.
2. Spray paint the outside.

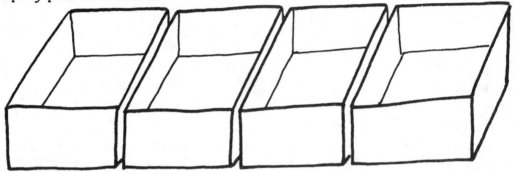

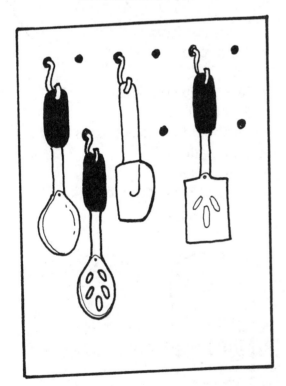

Mixing Center
Materials
- Large cardboard box
- S-hooks (from hardware store)
- Nail

Directions
1. Cut open box to lay flat.
2. Use the nail to make holes in the top half of the cardboard.
3. Insert S-hooks through the holes.
4. Stand cardboard behind mixing station table. Hang utensils on hooks.

☼ Center Enhancements

Ceiling Donuts

Materials
- Butcher paper
- Newspaper
- Stapler
- Yarn
- Scissors
- Tempera paint in assorted colors
- Paint brushes

Directions
1. Cut large donut shapes from butcher paper.
2. Place two together and staple the edges, leaving an opening.
3. Stuff lightly with newspaper. Staple the opening closed.
4. "Frost" the donuts with tempera paint (optional).
5. Securely staple a length of yarn to the donut. Hang from the ceiling over the center.

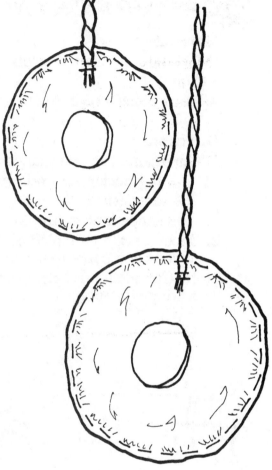

Wall Cookies

Materials
- Butcher paper
- Construction paper
- Glue
- Scissors
- Letter cut-outs

Directions
1. Cut large cookie shapes from butcher paper.
2. Glue construction paper to resemble chocolate chips, raisins, M & M's™ or other cookie ingredients.
3. Glue pre-cut or construction paper letters to the cookies to spell the center name.
4. Attach to the wall.

☀ Props to Make

☀ Cardboard Cookies

Materials
- Tagboard in assorted colors
- Glue
- Tissue paper or construction paper

Directions
1. Cut assorted cookie shapes from tagboard:
   - bar (rectangles and squares)
   - drop (circles)
   - shape (traced from cookie cutters)
2. Decorate with crumpled tissue paper or construction paper to resemble chocolate chips.

Note: Cut additional "plain" cookies for the decorating station.

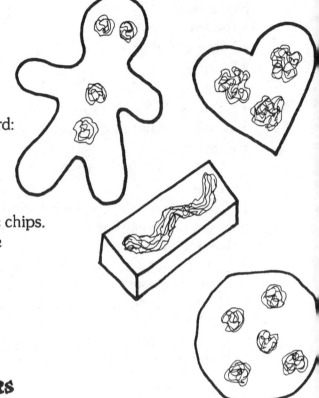

☀ Sniffers

Materials
- Assorted cooking spices—cinnamon, nutmeg, etc.
- Assorted extracts—lemon, vanilla, peppermint
- Cotton balls
- Pill bottles, with plastic caps*
- Ice pick

Directions
1. Remove the plastic caps. Use an ice pick to punch several holes in the cap.
2. Sprinkle a spice or extract on a cotton ball and place inside the bottle. Replace the lid.

*If plastic caps are not available, use netting secured with a rubber band to cover the opening.

40

PROPS TO MAKE

☀ COLORFUL CUPCAKES

Materials
- Paper baking cups
- Styrofoam™ balls, 2 inches (5 cm) in diameter
- Glue
- Spray paint in assorted colors

Directions
1. Spray paint top half of Styrofoam™ ball.
2. Glue in muffin cup.

☀ PASTRY PICTURES

Materials
- Used cookbooks that feature step-by-step baking illustrations
- Scissors   • Tagboard
- Glue

Directions
1. Cut apart sequential pictures.
2. Glue to tagboard. Number the backs in order.
3. Laminate.
4. Store in zip-top bags.

☀ LAYER CAKE

Materials
- Cake pattern (following page)
- White construction paper
- 3 x 16-inch (7.6 x 40.6 cm) strip of tagboard
- Glue
- Stapler

Directions
1. Reproduce and cut out cake pattern.
2. Glue two patterns, side-by-side, to paper strip, leaving 1-inch (2.54 cm) tab at one end.

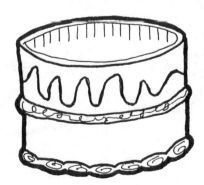

Note: Make additional "plain" cakes for the decorating center.

41

PROP PATTERN

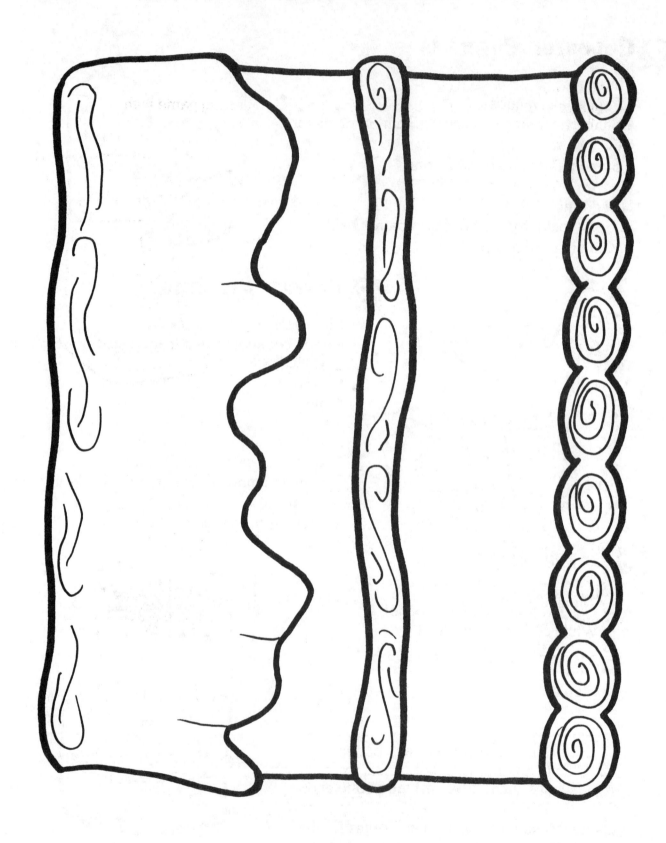

DEVELOPMENTAL ACTIVITIES

☺ SNIFFERS

Become smell detectives by sniffing the
spices and extracts in the bottle.

Skills To Build
• Sense development
• Vocabulary building
• Identifying relationships

☺ CAKE DECORATING

Combine real frosting with art supplies to
decorate layer cakes to sell at the counter.
Are any two cakes the same?

Skills To Build
• Small motor
• Creative expression
• Comparing and contrasting
• Color identification

45

LITERATURE LIST

PICTURE BOOKS

• *Chocolate Chip Cookies*
by Karen Wagner;
Henry Holt 1990. (PS-2)
This picture book takes youngsters through baking cookies.

• *Happy Easter Day!*
by Wendy Watson;
Houghton 1993. (PS-2)
A family prepares for Easter by participating in such activities as baking hot-cross buns.

• *The Stingy Baker*
by Janet Greeson;
Carolrhoda 1990. (PS-3)
A witch demands 13 cookies from a baker, supposedly the origin of a baker's dozen.

• *Benny Bakes a Cake*
by Eve Rice;
Greenwillow LB 1993. (PS-3)
On Benny's birthday, his mother allows him to bake a cake.

• *Sofie's Role*
by Amy Heath;
Macmillan 1992. (PS-2)
On the day before Christmas, a young girl helps her parents in their bakery.

• *Ruth's Bake Shop*
by Kate Spohn;
Orchard LB 1990. (K-2)
Ruth, an octopus, spends a joyful day baking all kinds of goodies.

BOOKS TO READ ALOUD

• *Mr. Cookie Baker*
by Monica Wellington;
Dutton 1992. (PS-K)
Mr. Cookie Baker makes a batch of delicious cookies that he gives to children in his shop.

• *Mimi and the Biscuit Factory*
by Viveca Sundvall;
Farrar 1989. (K-2)
On a visit to a local bakery, Mimi almost drops her loose tooth in a vat of dough.

• *Cookies and Crutches*
by Judy Delton;
Dell paper 1988. (1-2)
Molly and her friends find out that baking at home isn't quite as easy as it looks.

• *The Baker's Dozen: A Colonial American Tale*
by Heather Forest;
Harcourt 1988. (PS-2)
When a baker refuses to give 13 cookies to a dozen, his baking is cursed.

• *Hedgehog Bakes a Cake*
by Maryann Macdonald;
Bantam Paper 1990. (K-2)
Mayhem results when Hedghog's friends help him bake a cake.

• *Arthur's Christmas Cookies*
by Lillian Hoban;
Harper LB 1972. (1-2)
Arthur decides to bake cookies for a Christmas present for his parents.

© Edupress   *Theme Centers for Dramatic Play*

RESOURCES & MORE

RESOURCES & RELATED ACTIVITIES

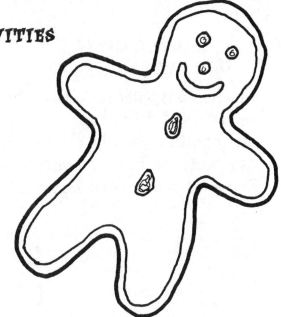

- Ask your local bakeries for a supply of cake and pastry boxes.

- Visit a local bakery.

- Introduce the concept of 12 and one dozen.

- Add candles to a Styrofoam™ birthday cake. Count the candles.

- Share cookbook pictures. Read recipe names and match the name to a picture.

- Decorate gingerbread men and "write" a group story about a ginger-cookie adventure.

- Invite a baker to demonstrate cake decorating.

- Make a chart showing the different shapes found in a bakery.

- Count the number of bread slices in a loaf; then make peanut butter sandwiches for snack time.

- Introduce the concepts of "before" and "after" with simple experiments:
    - Beat an egg white until it forms peaks.
    - Mix yeast with flour and water. Set the mixture aside to rise.
    - Make cookie dough. Bake the dough.

- Plan a cookie sampling session. Divide into groups by favorite cookie. Count the group members.

47

Dear Parents:

   We are preparing a Sweet Stuff Bakery Theme Center in our classroom during these dates: _____. This center will provide an opportunity for the children to participate in dramatic play and will serve as a basis for classroom discussion and learning activities. Below you will find a list of items that we need to furnish the center:

☐ Shoe box   ☐ Canned frosting

☐ Cooking utensils   ☐ Peel & stick hooks

☐ Old cookbooks   ☐ Baking pans

☐ Flour   ☐ Aprons

☐ Plastic knives   ☐ _____

Please return the items checked below by _____.

   You can support the use of this center by talking to your child about the theme, planning family excursions related to the theme, or by sharing books that will provide your child with more information. A suggested literature list is available upon request.

Parent Name _____

Phone Number _____ ☐ I would love to help!

48

Theme Centers for Dramatic Play

Good Grooming Spot

49

CENTER SET-UP

FLOORPLAN

KEEP US CLEAN TABLE

COSTUME BOX

HAIR DRESSING AREA

DRESSING AREA

50

Theme Centers for Dramatic Play

CENTER SET-UP

☺ FURNISHINGS AND ACCESSORIES

Hair Dressing Area
- Hair Dryer (Bare-Budget Furnishings)
- Mop Tops (Props to Make)
- Combs
- Brushes
- Barrettes & other hair accessories
- Snippy Scissors (Props to Make)

Keep Us Clean Table
- Bar soap
- Paper Towels
- Nail brushes
- Toothbrushes
- Plastic containers or tub

Dressing Area
- Dress-up Doll (Bare-Budget Furnishings)
- Shoe Shapes (Props to Make)
- Button Cards (Props to Make)
- Clothes Rack (page 206)
- Clothing for Dress-Up Doll

Costume Box
- Smocks
- Curly Coifs (Props to Make)
- Hats
- Large T-shirts
- Wigs
- Costume jewelry
- Gloves

51

BARE-BUDGET FURNISHINGS

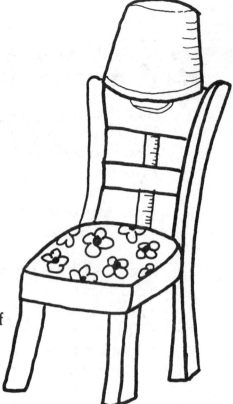

Hair Dryer
Materials
- Sturdy wooden or folding chair
- Wooden yardstick (meter stick)
- Duct tape
- 1-gallon (3.7 l) plastic ice cream container
- Contact paper

Directions
1. Cover ice cream container with contact paper.
2. Use duct tape to tape one end of yardstick inside of ice cream container.
3. Tape yardstick to back of wooden chair, adjusting to the proper height for children to sit under.

Dress-Up Doll
Materials
- 3 yards (2.74 m) muslin or other fabric
- Sewing machine **or** needle and thread
- Fiberfill™
- Yarn
- Fabric markers

Directions
1. Fold fabric in half lengthwise.
2. Cutting both layers of fabric at the same time, cut a child-size body outline.
3. Sew around figure, leaving an opening at the side. Turn.
4. Stuff with Fiberfill™. Stitch opening closed.
5. Sew strands of yarn on for hair and use fabric markers to draw a face.

52

Theme Centers for Dramatic Play

CENTER ENHANCEMENTS

Makeup Mirror

Cover a large tagboard circle with aluminum foil. Hot-glue a row of 2-inch (5 cm) Styrofoam™ balls around the edge to simulate light bulbs.

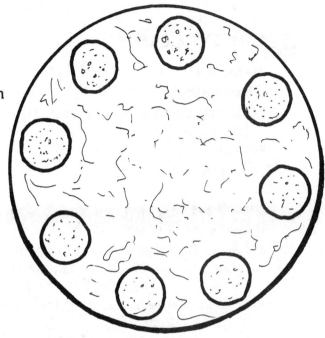

Super Smile

Use tagboard and markers to create a big "smile." Mount over Keep Us Clean Table.

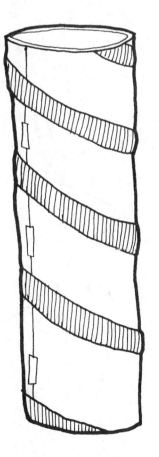

Barber Pole

Stack round ice cream containers and secure with duct tape. Cover with white butcher paper. Wrap a red crepe paper stripe around pole, securing with tape.

PROPS TO MAKE

CURLY COIFS

Materials
- Tagboard strip, 2 x 12 inches (5 x 30.5 cm)
- 2 sheets colored tissue paper, 10 x 20 inches (25.4 c 50.8 cm)
- Stapler
- Scissors
- Hole punch
- Yarn

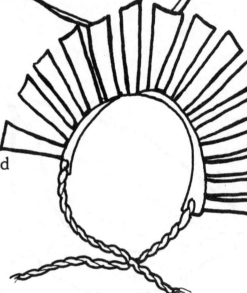

Directions
1. Stack tissue paper sheets.
2. Lay tagboard strip down the center of the paper, with edges of the tagboard extending beyond both edges of the tissue.
3. Fold the tissue in half over the tagboard strip. Staple securely.
4. Cut tissue into 1-inch (2.54 cm) strips, all the way to the tagboard.
5. Punch a hole in either end of tagboard strip and thread with yarn for tying under the chin.

SNIPPY SCISSORS

Materials
- Cardboard
- Large metal brad
- Exacto® knife
- Pencil

Directions
1. Trace two scissor shapes, as shown, on cardboard.
2. Cut out both shapes using the Exacto® knife.
2. Connect the shapes with brad.

54

Props to Make

Silly Shoes

Materials
- Shoe pattern (following page)
- Tagboard
- Shoe laces
- Hole punch
- Markers

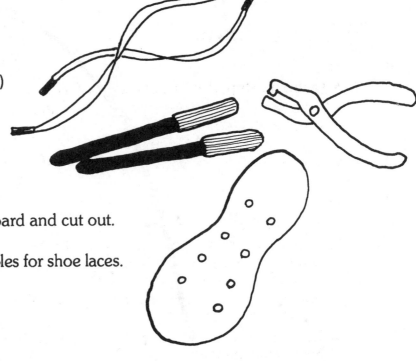

Directions
1. Trace shoe pattern on tagboard and cut out.
2. Decorate with markers.
3. Use hole punch to punch holes for shoe laces.

Button Cards

Materials
- Foam meat trays
- Large buttons with large holes
- Blunt needle
- Permanent marking pen

Directions
1. Use permanent marker to trace button shapes onto foam trays. Use buttons of the same size or vary the sizes, as desired.
2. Use blunt needle to poke thread holes into the center of button shapes.

55

PROP PATTERN

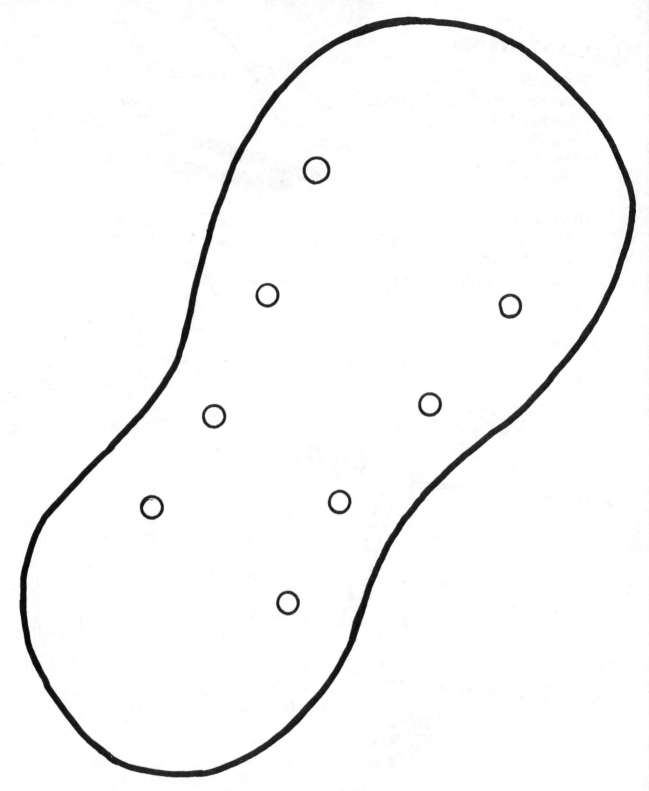

56

Theme Centers for Dramatic Play

CENTER TIPS

Introducing the Center
Read a selection from the literature list. Sing "This Is the Way We Wash Our Face," encouraging role-playing of different aspects of self-care and grooming.

Safety Tips
• Talk to children about not sharing combs and brushes.
• Remind children that belts and suspenders are for use on the Dress-Up Doll only.

CENTER VARIATIONS

Hat Shop
Stock the center with lots of different hats. Add hand mirrors, a sales counter, and cash register. Take turns being customers and sales people.

Beauty Salon
Enhance the "personal care" focus of the center by adding additional beauty care props and products such as:
- hand cream
- play makeup
- empty perfume bottles
- cardboard razor for shaving

57

Developmental Activities

Scrubbing Bubbles

Provide soap and containers of water near the nail brushes and toothbrushes to scrub up lots of bubbles.

Skills To Build
- Body awareness
- Sensory development
- Small motor skills

Button and Buckle

Provide child-size clothing for dressing the Dress-up Doll (Bare Budget Furnishings). Be sure to include belts, suspenders, and clothing with zippers, hooks and buttons.

Skills To Build
- Small motor skills
- Object identification
- Sequential movement

58

DEVELOPMENTAL ACTIVITIES

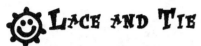

☼ LACE AND TIE

Provide Silly Shoes (Props to Make) and shoe laces. Encourage children to match pairs of shoes, learn to lace them and tie the shoe laces.

Skills To Build
- Small motor skills
- Visual discrimination
- Directionality

☼ BUTTON SEWING

Provide Button Cards (Props to Make), large buttons, and blunt plastic needles, already threaded with yarn and tied. Allow children to match buttons to cards and to attempt sewing the buttons to the cards.

Skills To Build
- Eye-hand coordination
- Directional vocabulary
- Visual discrimination
- Shape identification

59

Literature List

☼ Picture Books

• **One Bear in the Picture**
by Caroline Bucknall;
Puffin 1988. (PS-K)
Ted the bear is told by his mother to
keep his favorite outfit clean, which
he finds hard to do.

• **Molly**
by Ruth Radlauer;
Prentice 1987. (PS-K)
Scruffy Molly is set for school;
mother cleans her up, but she just
comes home messy again.

• **Marianna May and Nursey**
by Tomie dePaolo;
Holiday LB 1983. (PS-2)
Marianna May likes to get dirty, but
Nursey likes her to keep clean.

• **Dinosaurs Alive and Well! A
   Guide to Good Health**
by Laurene Krasney Brown & Marc
Brown;
Little 1990. (PS-3)
The basic principles of nutrition and
good hygiene are introduced.

• **Cornrows**
by Camille Yarbrough;
Putnam 1981. (1-3)
Past and present mingle in this
discussion of an unusual hairstyle.

• **Straight Hair, Curly Hair**
by Augusta Goldin;
Harper LB 1966. (1-3)
A very simple explanation of the
composition/characteristics of hair.

☼ Books to Read Aloud

• **Keeping Clean**
by Vicki Cobb;
Harper LB 1989. (1-3)
Stresses the importance of good
grooming.

• **Camilla's New Hairdo**
by Tricia Tusa;
Farrar 1991. (PS-3)
In her isolated tower, Camilla
fashions her long hair into the
shapes of the animals she sees.

• **Mrs. Pig Gets Cross and Other
   Stories**
by Mary Rayner;
Dutton 1987. (2-3)
Seven stories of Mrs. Pig and her
untidy piglets.

• **Murgatroyd's Garden**
by Judy Davos;
St. Martin's 1988. (PS-1)
Murgatroyd won't get his hair
washed, until finally a garden begins
to grown in it.

• **Theodore**
by Edward Ormondroyd;
Independence paper 1978. (PS-2)
A toy bear gets washed clean, and
his little girl owner doesn't recognize
him until he's properly dirty again.

• **Palm Trees**
by Nancy Cote;
Macmillan 1993. (PS-2)
Renne makes fun of Millie's
hairstyle, but in time tries it herself.

60

RESOURCES & RELATED ACTIVITIES

- Check the local thrift shop for a supply of hats and gloves.

- Invite a stylist or barber to come to class to give a haircut.

- Take a field trip to a barber shop and/or hair styling salon.

- Have a "dirtiest hands" contest. Let the children get dirty, and then have fun scrubbing up!

- Award each child a "Good Grooming Certificate" after giving them a chance to spiff up!

- Provide grooming checklists to be taken home. Provide a reward for charts that are completed and returned.

- Provide magazine pictures of clothing, construction paper and glue sticks. Have children design outfits.

- Have a relay race! Put clothing in two bags and have relayers see who can put the outfits on more quickly!

- Have some good grooming sensory and tactile experiences:
  - smell the difference in hand lotions or perfumes
  - apply hand lotion
  - rub the skin with different texture brushes and towels.

- Develop the concept of before and after:
  - give a wig a "haircut"
  - examine dirty and cleaned hands
  - paint fingernails, then remove with polish remover

Dear Parents:

We are preparing a Good Grooming Spot Theme Center in our classroom during these dates: _____. This center will provide an opportunity for the children to participate in dramatic play and will serve as a basis for classroom discussion and learning activities. Below you will find a list of items that we need to furnish the center:

☐ Hand mirrors   ☐ Children's clothing

☐ Old brushes   ☐ Wig stands

☐ Toothbrushes   ☐ Smocks

☐ Wigs   ☐ Hair accessories

☐ Barrettes   ☐ _____

Please return the items checked below by _____.

You can support the use of this center by talking to your child about the theme, planning family excursions related to the theme, or by sharing books that will provide your child with more information. A suggested literature list is available upon request.

Parent Name _____

Phone Number _____ ☐ I would love to help!

KID SHIP

Edupress   *Theme Centers for Dramatic Play*

CENTER SET-UP

FLOORPLAN

SHIP'S GALLEY

WATER TABLE

FISHING DECK

CAPTAIN'S QUARTERS

64

Center Set-Up

Furnishings and Accessories

Miscellaneous
- Mop
- Long rope to coil
- Life preserver or inflated inner tubes
- Blocks
- Captain's Wheel (Bare-Budget Furnishings)
- Wooden Plank (12" x 36"/30 cm x 91 cm)

Water Table
- Plastic tub
- Box filled with a variety of objects that sink or float (Activity Page— Making Waves)
- Container of sponge fish (Props to Make)
- Container of items for water stirring (Activity Page— Making Waves)

Costume Box
- Sailor hats
- Rubber boots
- Pirate hat
- Bandanas
- Snorkel
- Swim mask
- Swim fins
- Eye patches
- Swords
- Boots
- Swimming trunks and suits

Ship's Galley
- Play food

Fishing Deck
- Throw rug or carpet squares
- Fishing poles (Props to Make)
- Large plastic tub filled with fish (Props to Make)

Captain's Quarters
- Bookshelf
- Binoculars (Props to Make)
- Picture Books
- Bucket of rope lengths for knot-tying
- Ship-to-Shore Radio (Props to Make)
- Compass

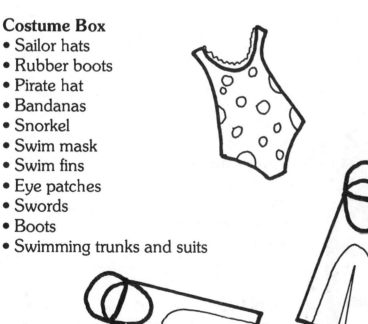

CENTER SET-UP

BARE-BUDGET FURNISHINGS

Captain's Wheel

Materials
- Tacky glue
- Two cardboard circles, approximately 18 inches (46 cm) in diameter
- Craft sticks
- Large metal brad
- Large cardboard box
- Markers

Directions
1. Glue craft sticks at intervals between cardboard circles.
2. Use metal brad to attach the wheel to the cardboard box.
3. Decorate with markers.

Costume Box

Materials
- Tempera paint
- Brown cardboard box
- Marking pens

Directions
1. Use paint and marking pens to decorate box to resemble treasure chest or tackle box.

66

CENTER SET-UP

CENTER ENHANCEMENTS

Ocean Waves

Cut waves from blue butcher paper. Sponge-paint the tips with white tempera to make whitecaps.

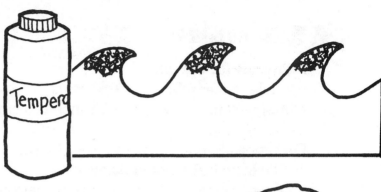

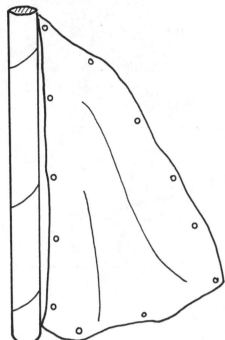

Wall Sails

Tack a white sheet to the wall to create a sail shape(s). Roll brown butcher paper to create masts.

Portholes

Cut white paper circles. Paint an "ocean scene" as viewed through a boat's porthole. This could be an art activity for the children.

Anchor

Cut an anchor from cardboard. Create a paper chain and attach to the anchor.

PROPS TO MAKE

☀ BINOCULARS

Materials for one pair
- 2 toilet paper tubes
- Masking tape
- Scissors
- 18-inch (46 cm) length of yarn

Directions
1. Place the tubes side-by-side.
2. Tape them together by wrapping masking tape several times around the outside.
3. Tape a yarn end to the outside of each tube so that the binoculars can be worn around the neck.

☀ SHIP-TO-SHORE RADIO

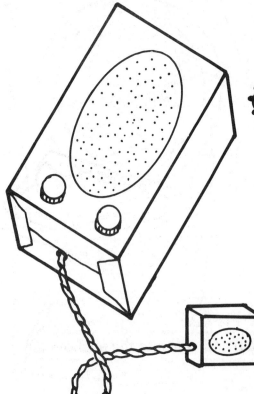

Materials
- Shoe box
- Marking pen
- Yarn
- Small gift box
- Contact paper

Directions
1. Cover the shoe box with contact paper.
2. Draw a "speaker" on both boxes.
3. Poke a hole in each box. Put an end of a yarn length through each hole. Tie a knot in the yarn ends to hold in place.

68

PROPS TO MAKE

PAPER FISH

Materials
- Scissors
- Magnetic tape
- Pencil
- Permanent marker
- Tagboard in a variety of colors
- Fish patterns, following

Directions
1. Cut out fish patterns.
2. Trace the patterns on tagboard and decorate with permanent marker.
3. Cut a strip of magnetic tape to adhere to one side of each fish.

FISHING POLE

Materials
- Paper clip
- Yarn
- 12-inch (30.5 cm) dowel

Directions
1. Tie one end of yarn length to paper clip.
2. Tie the other end of yarn length to dowel.

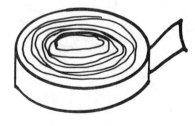

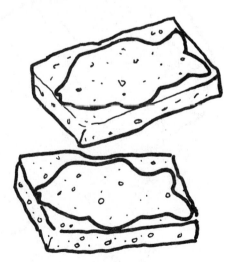

SPONGE FISH

Materials
- Fish patterns, following
- Marking pen
- Scissors
- 12 household sponges in 4 colors

Directions
1. Use the marking pen to trace a fish on each sponge.
2. Use scissors to cut out fish shapes.

Prop Pattern

70

Theme Centers for Dramatic Play

TEACHING TIPS

☼ CENTER TIPS

Introducing the Center
During circle time imagine you are on a ship. Rock back and forth. Introduce pictures of different kinds of boats.

Safety Tips
• Practice handling the fishing poles to prevent a child being poked with the end.
• Demonstrate "walking the plank." Determine the number of children to be allowed on the plank at one time.
• Discuss rope safety and establish rules regarding the coiled rope and rope pieces.

☼ CENTER VARIATIONS

Cruise Ship
• Add a game center that includes beach balls and shuffleboard.
• Place size-appropriate deck chairs and a chaise lounge.

Pirate Ship
• Make a pirate flag to fly over the boat.
• Read aloud from *Peter Pan*.

Submarine
• Add a goldfish bowl or aquarium.
• Introduce underwater life.
• Make crepe paper seaweed to hang from the ceiling.

Ⓔ Edupress   *Theme Centers for Dramatic Play*

DEVELOPMENTAL ACTIVITIES

FISHBOWL FUN

Stack, match, pattern, and play with fish shapes.

Skills To Build
- Sensory development
- Small motor skills
- Visual discrimination
- Patterning

FISHING

Stand "on deck" and drop a fishing pole "overboard." Reel in several fish. Count, match and sort.

Skills To Build
- Counting
- Visual discrimination
- Color recognition

72

Theme Centers for Dramatic Play

DEVELOPMENTAL ACTIVITIES

WALK THE PLANK

Walk backwards and forwards from one end of the wooden plank to the other.

Skills To Build
- Large motor development
- Directionality
- Spatial awareness
- Balance

MAKING WAVES

- Use scoops, wooden spoons, stirrers, and squirters to create water movement.
- Experiment with objects that sink and float.

Skills To Build
- Observation
- Eye-hand coordination
- Cause-and-effect associations
- Directionality

73

Theme Centers for Dramatic Play

LITERATURE LIST

PICTURE BOOKS

• **Boats**
by Ken Robbins;
Scholastic 1989. (PS-2)
Different boats are introduced
through photos and simple
descriptions.

• **Beach Ball**
by Peter Sis;
Greenwillow LB 1990. (PS-3)
A day at the beach brings scenes
that offer different activities.

• **The Story of the Seashore**
by John S. Goodall;
Macmillan 1990. (K-3)
This is a wordless picture book
about coastal life.

• **A Thousand Yards of Sea: A
Collection of Sea Stories and
Poems**
by Laura Cecil, ed.;
Greenwillow 1993. (PS-3)
A collection of poems exploring
various aspects of the sea.

• **Ocean**
by Ron Hirschi;
Bantam 1991. (PS-1)
Introduction to the ocean
environment and animals.

• **Sea Animals**
by Angela Royston;
Macmillan 1992. (PS-1)
Marine animals are identified
through full-color photographs.

BOOKS TO READ ALOUD

• **Old Hannibal and the Hurricane**
by Berthe Amoss;
Hyperion LB 1991. (K-2)
To escape a terrible hurricane, Old
Hannibal attaches wings to his
rowboat.

• **Emily and the Golden Acorn**
by Ian Beck;
Simon & Schuster 1992. (K-2)
Emily's favorite oak tree is
transformed into a sailing ship.

• **Alvin the Pirate**
by Ulf Lofgren;
Carolrhoda LB 1990. (1-3)
While digging for treasure in the
sand, Alvin is confronted with a
band of pirates who want him for
their captain.

• **The Pigrates Clean Up**
by Steven Kroll;
Henry Holt 1993. (K-3)
A boatload of pig pirates clean up
their ship and themselves for the
captain's wedding.

• **Why the Tides Ebb and Flow**
by Joan Chase Bowden;
Houghton 1979. (1-3)
In her search for a hut, Old Woman
causes the tides.

• **Come Away from the Water,
Shirley**
by John Burningham;
Harper LB 1977. (K-2)
While her parents nap on the beach,
Shirley goes adventuring at sea—in
her imagination.

74

RESOURCES & MORE

RESOURCES & RELATED ACTIVITIES

- Find travel posters featuring cruise lines.

- Invite a representative from the merchant marines or navy to speak about his job.

- Play tapes or records of nautical music.

- Ask for materials from a marine study center or aquarium.

- Talk about water sports. Share pictures of people waterskiing or participating in other water sports.

- Invite a local fisherman to tell stories about an adventure at sea.

- Visit a pet store to look at fish and aquariums.

- Arrange a field trip to visit a Coast Guard or Harbor Patrol office. Ask for a ride on the fireboat and a demonstration of their equipment.

- Learn to sing a sea shanty.

- Simulate these boating situations:
  - rowboat
  - high seas
  - raising a sail
  - reeling in a huge fish

- Invite a parent to demonstrate the use of a fishing pole.

- Bring in some fishing bait for children to handle; e.g., sardines, anchovies.

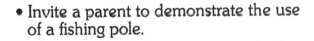

75

Dear Parents:

We are preparing a Kid Ship Theme Center in our classroom during these dates: _____. This center will provide an opportunity for the children to participate in dramatic play and will serve as a basis for classroom discussion and learning activities. Below you will find a list of items that we need to furnish the center:

☐ Toilet paper tubes

☐ Household sponges

☐ Yarn

☐ Magnetic tape

☐ Snorkel

☐ 12-inch (30 cm) wooden dowel

☐ Bandana

☐ Swim mask

☐ Swim fins

☐ _____

Please return the items checked above by _____.

You can support the use of this center by talking to your child about the theme, planning family excursions related to the theme, or by sharing books that will provide your child with more information. A suggested literature list is available upon request.

Parent Name _____

Phone Number _____ ☐ I would love to help!

CHILDREN'S
Shoes

Theme Centers for Dramatic Play

CENTER SET-UP

FLOORPLAN

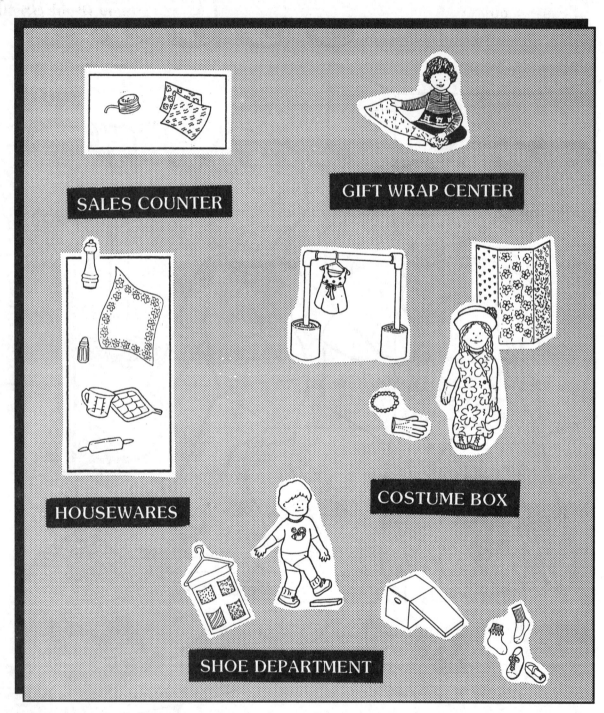

SALES COUNTER

GIFT WRAP CENTER

HOUSEWARES

COSTUME BOX

SHOE DEPARTMENT

Furnishings And Accessories

Sales Counter

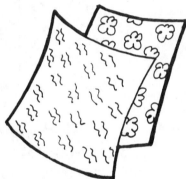

- Receipt books
- Empty gift boxes
- Ribbon
- Tape
- Shopping Bags (Props to Make)
- Gift cards
- Gift bags
- Tissue paper
- Box of old receipts
- Cans holding brushes, pencils, colored pencils, rulers, scissors

Gift Wrap Center

- Butcher paper
- Ribbon
- Boxes
- Tape
- Crayons
- Scissors

Costume Box

- Clothing Rack (Bare-Budget Furnishings)
- Fitting Room Screen (Bare-Budget Furnishings)
- Mirrors
- Dresses
- Shirts
- Jackets
- Skirts
- Belts
- Hats
- Purses
- Gloves
- Box of jewelry

Shoe Department (Book Shelf)

- Shoe boxes with shoes
- Shoe Bags (Props to Make)
- Socks
- Slippers

Housewares (Kitchen Unit)

- Cups and saucers
- Plates
- Pots and pans
- Silverware
- Cookbooks
- Wooden utensils in crock
- Salt and pepper shakers

79

Theme Centers for Dramatic Play

CENTER SET-UP

BARE-BUDGET FURNISHINGS

Fitting Room Screen
Materials
- Large appliance box
- Wallpaper samples
- Glue or rubber cement
- Scissors

Directions
1. Cut the top, bottom, and one side off the large box.
2. Cover with wallpaper samples to decorate. Stand upright, as shown.

Clothing Rack
Materials
- 9 feet (2.74 m) of PVC pipe
- 2 PVC right angle joints
- Sand
- Two plastic 5-gallon (18.5 l) ice cream tubs

Directions
1. Cut PVC pipe into three 3-foot (.9 m) lengths.
2. Connect with elbow fittings, as illustrated.
3. Secure pipes in ice cream tubs filled with sand.

Theme Centers for Dramatic Play

Center Enhancements

Mirrors

If no mirror is available to set out in clothing department, use a 4 x 2-foot (1.22 m x 61 cm) piece of cardboard covered with aluminum foil (shiny side up), stapled or taped to secure. Make 1 x 1-foot (30 x 30 cm) size for shoe department. To the back of each add two triangular pieces of cardboard at right angles to act as supports. Secure with tape.

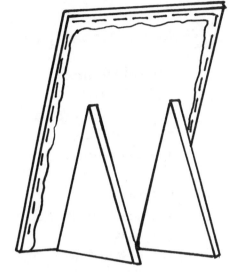

Department Display Signs

Use tagboard to create individual department signs. Illustrate each sign depicting items that are sold there.

Table Cloth for Housewares Table

Use a large square of muslin and decorate border with stencil or sponge paint design. Use as a table cloth in the housewares area.

Shoe Stools

Nail a thin piece of plywood to the front edge of a low stool or box. The plywood should be cut the width of the stool seat and long enough to reach the floor, as shown.

Props to Make

☀ Shoe Size Measure

Materials
- Paint stirrer
- Permanent markers
- Cardboard
- Tacky glue
- Styrofoam™
- Masking tape
- Scissors

Directions
1. Mark ½-inch (1.27 cm) intervals on paint stirrer, using markers.
2. Cut a wedge of Styrofoam™ as shown above. Cut a second piece of Styrofoam™. Glue to end of paint stirrer.
3. Cut a piece of cardboard strip, 1 inch (2.54 cm) wide.
4. Wrap the cardboard around the width of the paint stirrer, securing it with masking tape to form a cuff.
5. Glue Styrofoam™ wedge to cardboard cuff and slide over end of paint stirrer.

☀ Shoe Bag

Materials
- Wire clothes hanger
- Canvas, cut 12 x 24 inches (30 x 61 cm)
- Fabric squares (5 x 7 inches/12.7 x 17.8 cm)
- Tacky glue

Directions
1. Fold top 2 inches (5 cm) of canvas over hanger and glue in place.
2. Glue fabric squares to canvas, leaving top edges open.

Theme Centers for Dramatic Play

PROPS TO MAKE

FANCY FRAMES

Materials
- Frame pattern (following page)
- Tagboard
- Scissors
- Glue
- Sequins, shells or other craft materials
- Crayons

Directions
1. Trace pattern onto tagboard.
2. Cut around outside. Leave inside intact.
3. Decorate with crayons and craft materials.

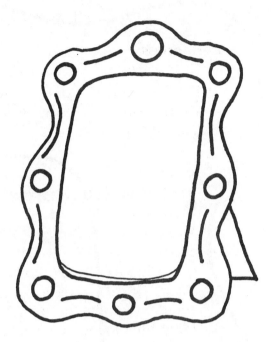

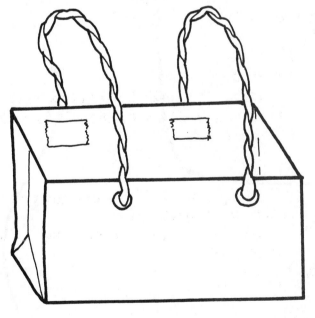

SHOPPING BAG

Materials
- Paper grocery bag
- Yarn
- Tape

Directions
1. Cut top half off grocery bag.
2. Punch two holes in each of two opposite sides of the bag.
3. Tie yarn to form a handle in each side.
3. Tape over yarn holes on inside to prevent tearing.

83

PROP PATTERN

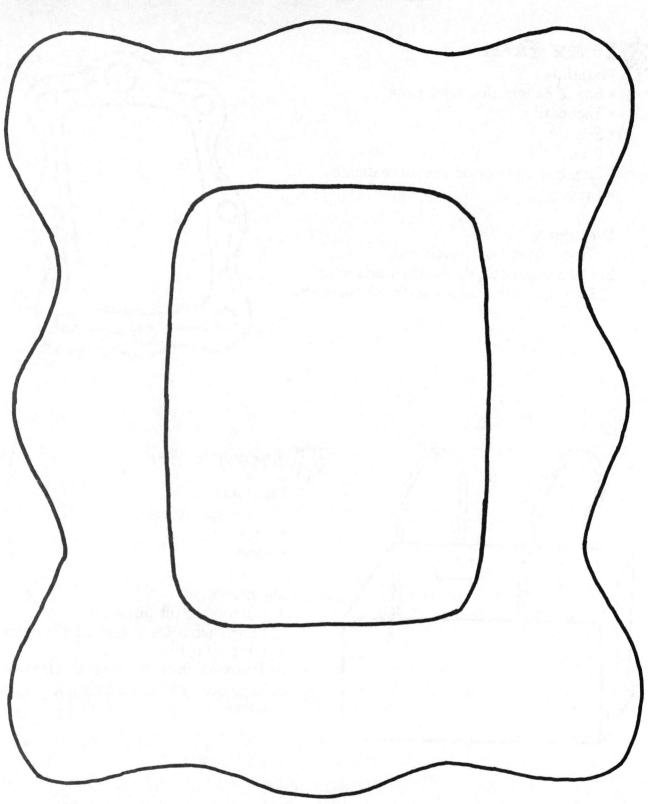

84

Theme Centers for Dramatic Play

CENTER TIPS

Introducing the Center
Go around the circle and ask each child if she/he is wearing anything new. Where did it come from? What was it like buying it? Did you have to try it on? What else did they sell at the store?

Safety Tips
• Only one child may use the shoe stool at a time.
• Only one child may use the fitting room at a time.
• The shoe measurer is to be used only to measure feet.

CENTER VARIATIONS

Baby Store
• Remove adult items and add baby shoes, socks, clothes and baby dishes to the center.
• Remove posters and add baby pictures to Fine Arts Department.
• Create a corner that is a photography studio with backdrop of blanket and toys. Add camera for picture-taking. Include pre-cut photo frames made of tagboard and put out old baby photos and albums.

Sporting Goods Store
• Add playground equipment, jogging shorts, sweat pants, and literature about sports.

85

DEVELOPMENTAL ACTIVITIES

SHOE MEASURING

Allow children to measure their feet with the
Shoe Size Measure (Props to Make) or make
a display of shoes and encourage the
children to arrange them according to size.

Skills To Build
- Comparing bigger and smaller
- Number concepts
- Seriation
- Enumerating objects

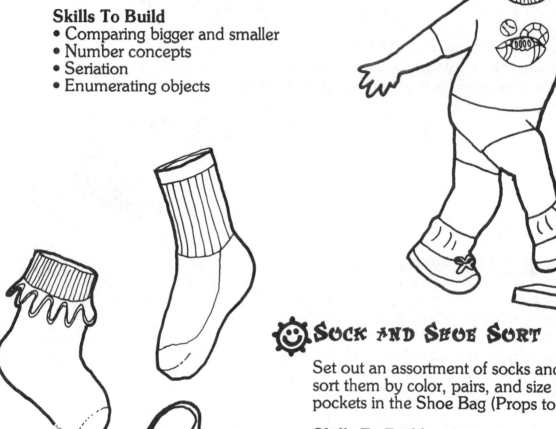

SOCK AND SHOE SORT

Set out an assortment of socks and shoes, then
sort them by color, pairs, and size into the
pockets in the Shoe Bag (Props to Make).

Skills To Build
- Visual discrimination
- Size comparison
- Color identification
- Sorting

86

DEVELOPMENTAL ACTIVITIES

☺ MAKE GIFT WRAP AND WRAP BOXES

Set out supplies to create gift wrap. Invite children to create their own. Gift wrap boxes.

Skills To Build
• Coloring
• Small motor
• Size discrimination

☺ FRAME CREATIONS

Set out Fancy Frames (Props to Make) in the Gift Wrap Center. Decorate frames with crayons and other materials to "sell" in Housewares.

Skills To Build
• Small motor
• Art expression

LITERATURE LIST

PICTURE BOOKS

• **Department Store**
by Gail Gibbons;
Harper paper 1984. (K-3)
A day in the life of a department
store.

• **Tom and Annie Go Shopping**
by Barry Smith;
Houghton 1989. (K-2)
Familiar objects are hidden in
extremely detailed pictures.

• **Lily and the Present**
by Christine Ross;
Houghton 1992. (PS-3)
Lily goes shopping for a present for
her new baby brother.

• **Laney's Lost Momma**
by Diane J. Hamm;
Whitman 1991 (PS-1)
Mother and daughter are reunited
after Laney loses her mother in a
department store.

• **Carl Goes Shopping**
by Alexandra Day;
Farrar Strauss Giroux 1989. (PS-1)
Carl and the baby in his care
explore the department store.

• **The Purse**
by Kathy Carple;
Houghton 1986. (PS-1)
Katie decides her new purse doesn't
"clunk" as well as her old Band-Aid
box did.

BOOKS TO READ ALOUD

• **The Wheels on the Bus**
by Maryann Kovalski;
Little 1987. (PS-2)
Grandmother takes her lookalike
granddaughters shopping and
teaches them a silly song.

• **Max's Dragon Shirt**
by Rosemary Wells;
Dial LB 1991. (PS-1)
Max and his rabbit sister Ruby
become separated when they go
shopping in a department store.

• **Amy Elizabeth Explores
Bloomingdale's**
by E.L. Konigsburg;
Macmillan 1992. (PS-2)
Amy visits her grandmother in New
York City and set out to explore.

• **The Go-Around Dollar**
by Barbara J. Adams;
Macmillan 1992. (2-4)
The dollar is introduced within the
framework of a story.

• **"No!" Said Joe**
by John Prater;
Candlewick 1992. (PS-1)
Joe's imaginative parents think of all
the things that might happen if he
does not come shopping with them.

• **The Big Green Pocketbook**
by Candice Ransom;
Harper LB 1993. (PS-2)
At every stop during a day of
errands with her mother, a little girl
is given something to put in her
empty pocketbook.

© Edupress   Theme Centers for Dramatic Play

RESOURCES & MORE

RESOURCES & RELATED ACTIVITIES

- Take a trip to a local department store.

- Invite a parent who works at a store to come and share some experiences.

- Send parent letter home—suggest parent and child plan a trip to the department store.

- After child has visited department store, draw a picture and dictate a story.

- Have the children each bring in an old baby shoe to see how much they've grown.

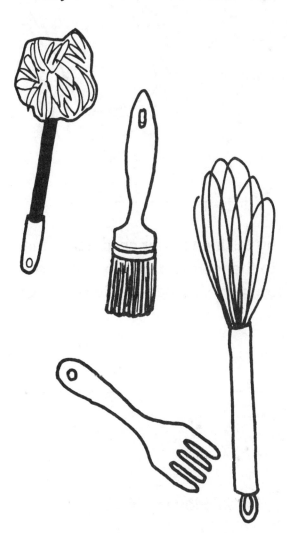

- Use a department store shopping bag to play a memory game. Pack the bag with several items as children watch. Ask them to list the items in the bag.

- Make a graph charting the baby shoes sizes brought to class.

- Send a parent letter asking for department store bags. Cut them into pieces and make a collage.

- Use different gadgets from the Housewares Department to do gadget painting.

- Conduct a comparison of what would be found in a grocery store, department store, and sporting goods store.

- Play a verbal game: "I'm going to the department store and I'm going to buy…" Children complete the sentence by drawing on personal experience. Alter the game by going to a grocery store.

Theme Centers for Dramatic Play

Dear Parents:

  We are preparing a Smart Shop Department Store Theme Center in our classroom during these dates: _____. This center will provide an opportunity for the children to participate in dramatic play and will serve as a basis for classroom discussion and learning activities. Below you will find a list of items that we need to furnish the center:

☐ Old jewelry   ☐ Department store bags

☐ Cookbooks   ☐ Salt & pepper shakers

☐ Baskets   ☐ Tissue paper

☐ Wooden utensils   ☐ Empty gift boxes

☐ Shoes in boxes   ☐ _____

Please return the items checked above by _____.

You can support the use of this center by talking to your child about the theme, planning family excursions related to the theme, or by sharing books that will provide your child with more information. A suggested literature list is available upon request.

Parent Name _____

Phone Number _____ ☐ I would love to help!

Playful Pet Shop

91

CENTER SET-UP

FLOORPLAN

PLAYFUL PET SHOP

CUTE CAT MAGAZINE

BOOK CASE

ART SHELF

PET SHELF

WORK TABLE

KITCHEN UNIT

COSTUME BOX

CENTER SET-UP

☀ FURNISHINGS AND ACCESSORIES

Art Shelf
- Animal Sponge Shapes (Props to Make)
- Animal rubber stamps
- Stamp pads
- Toilet paper tubes
- Magazines
- Collage items: feathers, fake fur, seeds, kibble, small dog bones
- Pie tins
- Tempera paint

Work Table
- Juice cans holding scissors, hole punches, pencils, colored pencils
- Dog biscuits
- Dapper Dogs (Props to Make)
- Bowls

Costume Box
- Variety of hats
- Variety of shoes
- Purses & tote bags
- Smocks
- Aprons
- Assorted shirts, dresses, skirts, pants
- Animal masks & costumes

Book Case
- Animal magazines
- Audobon Field Guides
- Animal care manuals featured in Book Display Rack (Bare-Budget Furnishings)

Kitchen Unit
- Assorted dishes for animals
- Containers of bird seed
- Variety of small containers
- Scale
- Aquarium (Center Enhancements)
- Fish Net (Props to Make)

Pet Shelf
- Cash register
- Play money
- Receipt book
- Bags for purchases
- Pet food cans
- Bird seed boxes
- Bin containing balls, dog bones, squeaky toys
- Animal magazines
- Hamster Cage (Bare-Budget Furnishings)

Drying Rack (page 206)
- Leashes
- Collars

93

CENTER SET-UP

BARE-BUDGET FURNISHINGS

Small Animal Cage
Materials
- Plastic dishpan
- Chicken wire (small grid)
- Florist wire
- Ice pick
- Kitchen shears/tin snips
- Masking tape

Directions
1. Measure perimeter of dishpan and purchase that amount of chicken wire, allowing enough to create a lid.
2. Cut chicken wire to conform to dishpan shape. Cut rectangle for lid.
3. Use ice pick to make holes in the lip on each side of the dishpan.
4. Secure wire top to dishpan with florist wire.
5. Cover all protruding edges of wire with masking tape.
6. Put small stuffed animal inside.

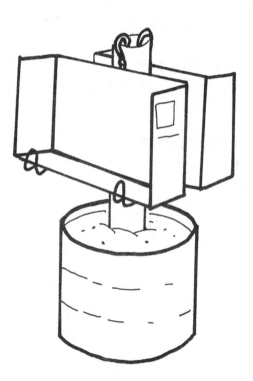

Book Display Rack
Materials
- 2 cereal boxes
- 2 wire coat hangers
- Coffee can filled with sand
- Butcher paper
- Paper towel tube

Directions
1. Cover cereal boxes with butcher paper and cut out front panel of each box.
2. Bend coat hangers to hold books:
   - bend hook toward the back
   - bend sides toward center one-half the distance from center
   - bend ends up.
3. Rest cardboard box on upturned arms.
4. Secure paper towel tube in sand-filled coffee can.
5. Put hooks of hangers into tube and secure with tape, flattening hooks as needed to stabilize.

94

Theme Centers for Dramatic Play

CENTER ENHANCEMENTS

Pets in Cages

Cut rectangles spaced about 2 inches (5.08 cm) apart from the sides of cardboard boxes. Place large stuffed animals in the boxes.

Playful Pet Shop

Use butcher paper to create a store name sign. Add pictures of animals cut from magazines.

Aquarium

Thoroughly wash out a 1-gallon (3.7 l) clear wide-mouth jar (plastic is best). Rinse repeatedly and allow to dry overnight. Fill with water and a variety of plastic fish.

PROPS TO MAKE

PET FOOD

Materials
- Paper bags and boxes in assorted sizes
- Newspaper
- Markers
- Butcher paper
- Stapler
- Tape

Directions
1. To make bags of pet food, fill paper bags with crumpled newspaper. Staple closed and decorate with markers.
2. Wrap boxes with butcher paper. Secure with tape and decorate with markers.

BUTTERFLY NET

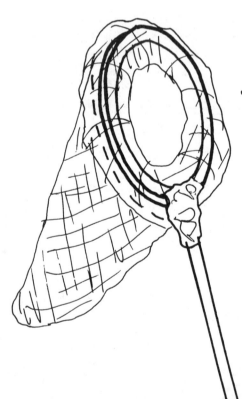

Materials
- Large coffee can lid
- ¼-inch (.6 cm) dowel, 24 inches (61 cm) long
- Needle and thread
- Scissors
- Tape
- Stapler
- Nylon net

Directions
1. Cut coffee can lid so that only the edge remains.
2. Secure dowel to lid with tape.
3. Place net over edge of lid, leaving center open. Secure with running stitch. (Net will hang down away from lid.)
4. Gather net below lid and staple together.

96

PROPS TO MAKE

 **DAPPER DOGS**

Materials
- Dog pattern (following page)
- White paper or construction paper
- Tagboard • Glue • Markers

Directions
1. Trace dog pattern several times onto white paper or construction paper. Cut out.
2. Use markers to fill in the details of each dog.
3. On left ear draw a selected number of dots.
4. On the right ear, write the numeral that corresponds with the dots on the left ear.
5. Glue dogs to large sheet of tagboard.

BIRD SHAPES

Materials
- Bird pattern (following page)
- Tagboard
- Scissors

Directions
1. Trace bird pattern onto tagboard. Cut out.
2. Store on art table with collage items.

97

98

Theme Centers for Dramatic Play

TEACHING TIPS

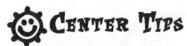

CENTER TIPS

Introducing the Center
Send a note home to the parents asking them to send a picture of their family pet. Include a fact sheet about name, age, variety, favorite food. Share during circle time.

Safety Tips
- Remind children that dog biscuits are not for eating.
- Tell children that dog toys are not children's toys.
- Remind children that leashes and collars are for dogs and cats only.

CENTER VARIATIONS

Grooming Parlor
Add animal grooming equipment (scissors, combs, towels, brushes) and empty bottles of dog shampoo.

Petting Zoo
Put stuffed sheep, pigs, rabbits and ducks in center. Add buckets filled with hay.

99

DEVELOPMENTAL ACTIVITIES

☼ Fish Scoop

Get your Fish Nets (Props to Make) out and scoop up some colorful fish out of the aquarium (Center Enhancements).

Skills To Build
- Counting
- Color identification
- Concept of floating & sinking

☼ Dog Biscuit Count

Put out Dapper Dogs (Props to Make) along with dog bowls and a box of dog biscuits. Encourage children to count bones into bowls.

Skills To Build
- Counting
- Number recognition
- Greater than, less than

100

Developmental Activities

☺ Measure and Weigh Bird Seed

Make bird seed, a variety of containers and a scale available. These may be used to measure and weigh the seeds. Put out zip-lock bags.

Skills To Build
- Acquiring skills with tools
- Comparing amounts
- Combing and sorting

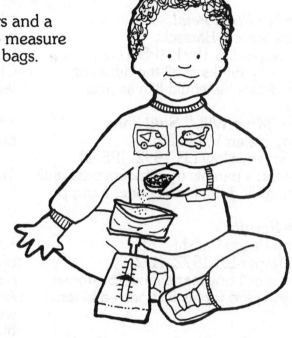

☺ Bone Pile

Make Dog Bones (Free Weights, page 278) and use them like building blocks to make a big bone pile.

Skills To Build
- Counting
- Balancing
- Spatial relations

LITERATURE LIST

PICTURE BOOKS

• *No Plain Pets!*
by Marc I. Barasch;
Harper LB 1991. (PS-1)
A boy thinks of all the different
animals he would like as pets.

• *"Mine Will," Said John*
by Helen V. Griffith;
Greenwillow LB 1992. (PS-3)
John's parents try different pets until
they find the perfect one, a puppy.

• *Scruffy*
by Peggy Parish;
Harper LB 1972. (1-2)
A small boy learns how to choose
and care for his first pet—a kitten.

• *Loving*
by Ann Morris;
Lothrop LB 1990. (PS-2)
Clear photos focus on children, their
families, and their pets.

• *Poonam's Pets*
by Andrew & Diana Davies;
Viking 1990. (PS-K)
The quietest child in first grade
brings "6 enormous lions" to school
on pet day.

• *A Bicycle for Rosaura*
by Daniel Barbot;
Kane-Miller 1991. (PS-1)
A pet store owner is in a quandary
when her hen Rosaura asks for a
bicycle for her birthday.

BOOKS TO READ ALOUD

• *Can I Keep Him?*
by Steven Kellogg;
Dial 1971. (K-2)
Arnold constantly distresses his
mother with a wide assortment of
pets—real, imaginary and human.

• *Furry*
by Holly Keller;
Greenwillow LB 1992. (PS-K)
Laura is allergic to all kinds of pets
except a chameleon.

• *No More Monsters for Me*
by Peggy Parish;
Harper LB 1981. (K-3)
A young girl wants to keep a
monster for a pet.

• *You're Not My Cat*
by Theresa Burns;
Harper LB 1990. (PS-2)
A stray cat comes into a little girl's
life, but only on his terms.

• *Our Puppy's Vacation*
by Ruth Brown;
Dutton 1987. (PS-1)
The fun of a first vacation for a
Labrador puppy.

• *The Take-Along Dog*
by Barbara Ann Porter;
Greenwillow LB 1989. (PS-3)
Their boisterous new pup won't
stay hidden in a beach bag, causing
headaches for Sam and Abigail.

RESOURCES & MORE

☺ RESOURCES & RELATED ACTIVITIES

- Visit a pet shop.

- Invite parents to bring in the family pet.

- Create a class library of animal books.

- Go on a class bug walk using bug jars and butterfly nets from the classroom.

- Play "Doggie, Doggie, Where's Your Bone?"
    - *Children sit in a circle with their hands behind their backs. One child sits in the center of the circle, eyes covered.*
    - *Dog biscuit is passed from child to child until teacher says, "Hide the bone."*
    - *Children chant: "Doggie, doggie, where's your bone? Somebaody took it from your home."*
    - *The "center" child approaches each child in the circle until he finds the biscuit. Child with biscuit replaces the child in the center.*

- Invite someone from local animal control to come and visit the class.

- Ask a snake owner to bring his pet "Boa" to class.

- Create animal masks to use while dancing and role-playing to Saen-Saint's *Carnival of the Animals.*

- Create a class pet list.

- Visit a pet store. Paint a large mural of the many pets you saw.

- Use brown paper bags to make pet puppets and role-play with them.

103

Dear Parents:

   We are preparing a Playful Pet Shop Theme Center in our classroom during these dates: _____. This center will provide an opportunity for the children to participate in dramatic play and will serve as a basis for classroom discussion and learning activities. Below you will find a list of items that we need to furnish the center:

☐ Pet food dishes   ☐ Animal magazines

☐ Leashes & collars   ☐ Empty pet food containers

☐ Pet owner manual   ☐ Plastic dishpan

☐ Pet toys   ☐ Plastic jars

☐ Dog biscuits   ☐ _____

   Please return the items checked above by _____.

   You can support the use of this center by talking to your child about the theme, planning family excursions related to the theme, or by sharing books that will provide your child with more information. A suggested literature list is available upon request.

Parent Name _____

Phone Number _____   ☐ I would love to help!

Little Folks' Library

STORY HOUR

READ A BOOK

CURL UP WITH A Good Book!

Puppet Fun

BOOKS TO BE SORTED

105

Theme Centers for Dramatic Play

Center Set-Up

☼ Floorplan

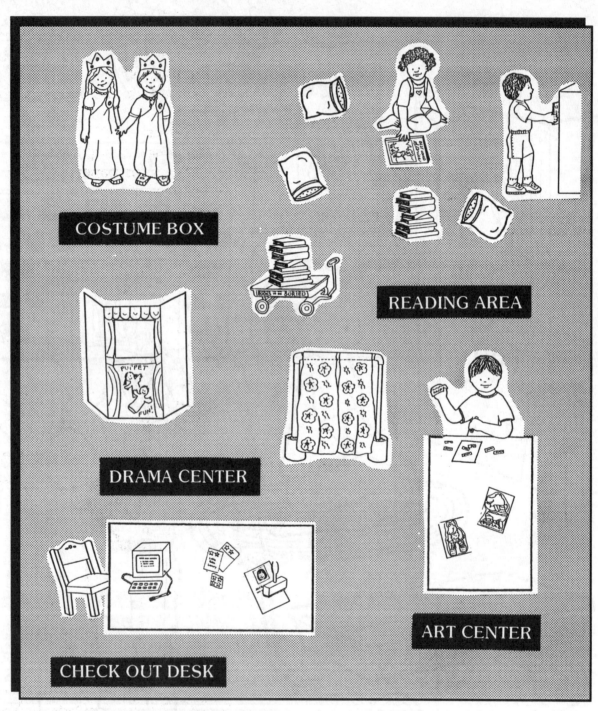

COSTUME BOX

READING AREA

DRAMA CENTER

ART CENTER

CHECK OUT DESK

☀ Furnishings And Accessories

Reading Area
- Bookshelves
- Picture books
- Magazines
- Floor pillows
- Tape recorder & story tapes
- Book wagon or utility cart

Check-Out Desk
- Library Cards (Props to Make)
- Library Pockets (Props to Make)
- Rubber stamps & stamp pads
- Hole punch
- Date Stamp
- Computer Terminal (Bare-Budget Furnishings)
- Book bags
- Small box for library card storage

Costume Box
- Crown (Props to Make)
- Pirate hats
- Dresses
- Scarves
- Coats
- Hats
- Costumes

Drama Center
- Stick Puppets (Props to Make)
- Puppet Theater (Bare-Budget Furnishings)
- Story Prompt Books (Props to Make)

Art Center
- Magazines, newspapers
- Construction paper
- Scissors

107

CENTER SET-UP

BARE-BUDGET FURNISHINGS

Computer Terminal

Materials
- Cardboard box, 18 inches (45.72 cm) square
- Construction paper square, approximately 15 inches (38 cm) square
- Shoe box lid
- Small flashlight
- Yarn
- Glue
- Markers

Directions
1. Glue construction paper to the front of cardboard box.
2. Use markers to create a typewriter keyboard on top of shoe box lid.
3. Cut one length of yarn. Punch holes in the large box and on the side of shoe box lid. Tie one end of yarn to box, the other end to the box lid.
4. Cut a second strand of yarn. Punch another hole in cardboard box. Tie one end of yarn to box, the other end around the end of the flashlight.

Puppet Theater

Materials
- Large appliance box or voting booth
- Exacto® knife
- Markers

Directions
1. Use Exacto® knife to cut off one side and top and bottom flaps of appliance box.
2. Set box or voting booth upright. Cut opening in front of box.
3. Decorate box with markers.

108

CENTER ENHANCEMENTS

Story Hour

Use markers or tempera paint and tagboard to create a large clock face. Decorate the clock with the words "Story Hour." Mount on the wall.

Fireplace

Paint a brick fireplace with a fire in it on butcher paper. Mount it on wall near the reading area.

Sorting Cart

Use tagboard to make a sign reading "Books to be Sorted." Tape to a wheeled utility cart or children's wagon.

PROPS TO MAKE

LIBRARY CARDS

Materials
- 3 x 5-inch (7.6 x 12.7 cm) index cards, 1 for each student plus ten additional
- Individual student pictures
- Glue
- Stickers
- Library pockets (available at stationery store)

Directions
1. Glue one student picture to each card.
2. Put a different sticker(s) on each of the remaining ten cards. Put a matching sticker(s) on each of the ten library pockets.
3. If desired, print the name of library center on card.
4. Store in a box at Check-Out Desk.

Little Folks Library

STICK PUPPETS

Materials
- "People" or "animal" pictures
- Paint stirrers or tongue depressors
- Tagboard
- Glue

Directions
1. Select pictures of people or animals from magazines. Glue to tagboard and cut out.
2. Glue pictures to ends of paint stirrers or tongue depressors.
3. Store in a container near the Puppet Theater.

110

Props to Make

Story Prompt Books

Materials
- Magazine pictures
- Large sheets of construction paper
- Glue

Directions
1. Select large illustrations of people and animals involved in a variety of activities in a variety of places.
2. Cut construction paper in half lengthwise then accordion-fold into three equal sections.
3. Glue a magazine picture to each section. Laminate, if desired.

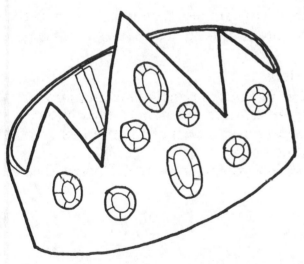

Crown

Materials
- Crown pattern (following page)
- Tagboard
- Scissors
- Aluminum foil
- Plastic "jewels"
- Glue
- Tape

Directions
1. Use pattern to make crown shape o tagboard.
2. Cover with aluminum foil.
3. Glue jewels to crown front to decorate.
4. Tape ends together to fit head.
5. Place in costume box for role-playing.

PROP PATTERN

PLACE ON FOLD

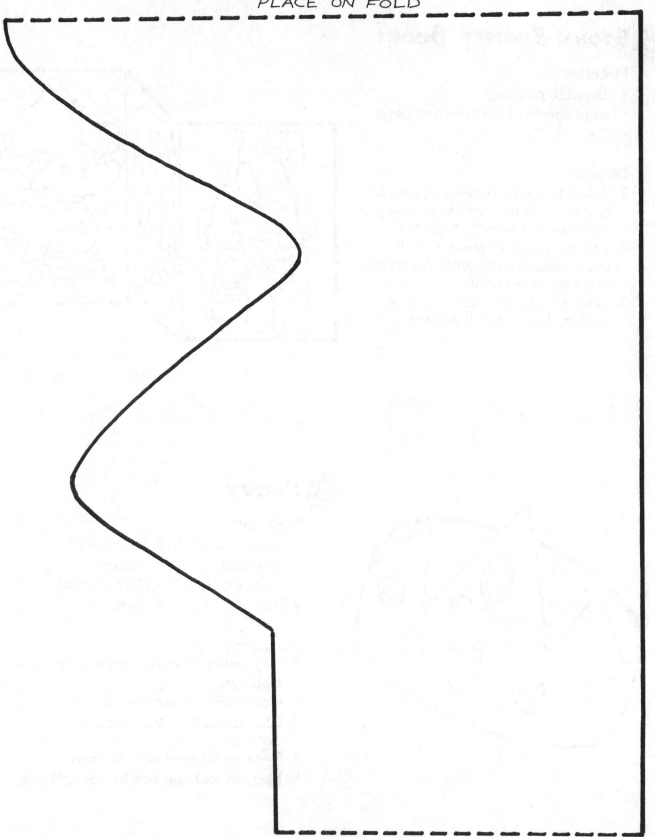

112

ADD 1" HERE

Theme Centers for Dramatic Play

TEACHING TIPS

☺ CENTER TIPS

Introducing the Center
During circle time introduce a stack of new picture books in a book bag. Read a story, then role-play taking a walk and entering the library. Discuss the concepts of lending, borrowing, and sharing.

☺ CENTER VARIATIONS

Book Store
Turn the Check-Out Desk into a store counter with a cash register and shopping bags. Provide play money. Encourage children to bring books to "trade."

Children's Theater
Create a curtain by taping cloth to an arch constructed from PVC pipe secured in large coffee containers filled with sand. "Stage" reenactments of favorite children's literature.

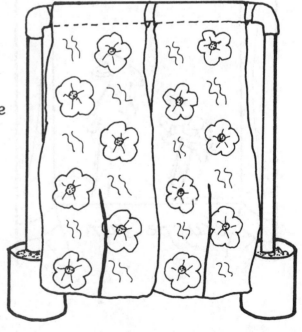

Theme Centers for Dramatic Play

DEVELOPMENTAL ACTIVITIES

CHECK IT OUT

Use date stamps, rubber stamps, stamp pads and hole punches to "check out" books on individual library cards (Props to Make).

Skills To Build
- Calendar awareness
- Visual discrimination
- Color identification

THEATER PLAY

Use Story Prompt Books (Props to Make) and Stick Puppets (Props to Make) to encourage presentations in the puppet theater.

Skills To Build
- Sequencing
- Role-playing
- Creative thinking

DEVELOPMENTAL ACTIVITIES

WORD COLLAGE

Provide sheets of newspaper, magazines, and pieces of construction paper at art table. Make collages of words.

Skills To Build
- Letter seqencing
- Letter recognition
- Differentiating between words and pictures

FILL A POCKET

Match library cards to library pockets. Put the card inside the pocket.

Skills To Build
- Visual discrimination
- Matching
- Patterning

115

LITERATURE LIST

PICTURE BOOKS

• **How My Library Grew by Dinah**
by Martha Alexander;
Wilson 1983. (PS-K)
Dinah and her teddy bear watch a
library being built across the street.

• **Sophie and Sammy's Library
Sleepover**
by Judith Casely;
Greenwillow 1992. (PS-2)
With the help of older sister Sophie,
Sammy learns to love and respect
books.

• **Check It Out: The Book About
Libraries**
by Gail Gibbons;
Harcourt 1985. (K-3)
A picture-book overview of what the
library is and how it functions.

• **I Took My Frog to the Library**
by Eric A. Kimmel;
Viking 1990. (PS-K)
A number of different animals create
havoc when they visit the library.

• **Aunt Lulu**
by Daniel Pinkwater;
Macmillan 1988. (PS-1)
Aunt Lulu the librarian owns 14
Huskies and delivers library books
in Alaska.

• **Let's Go to the Library**
by Lisl Weil;
Holiday 1990. (1-4)
This history of libraries and books
contains many illustrations.

BOOKS TO READ ALOUD

• **How a Book is Made**
by Aliki;
Harper LB 1986. (K-3)
Cat people play all the parts in this
minimal text account of how picture
books are made.

• **The Day the TV Blew Up**
by Dan West;
Whitman LB 1988. (1-3)
Ralph's TV blows up, and his friend
Thelma suggest he go to the library,
where they loan books "for free."

• **Tell Me Some More**
by Crosby Bonsall;
Harper LB 1961. (1-3)
Andrew introduces his friend to the
magic of the library.

• **Armondo Asked, "Why?"**
by Jay Hulbert;
Raintree LB 1990. (K-3)
Armando asks so many tough
questions that the family has to go
to the library to find the answers.

• **Harry in Trouble**
by Barbara Ann Porte;
Greenwillow LB 1989. (1-3)
Harry's third library card has
disappeared.

• **Walter's Magic Wand**
by Eric Houghton;
Watts LB 1977. (K-3)
In a library, Walter creates havoc
with a magic wand that opens up
the wonders found in books.

RESOURCES & MORE

RESOURCES & RELATED ACTIVITIES

- Arrange a field trip to the local library, including a story hour.

- Make story books on pre-cut construction paper. Have children dictate their stories to an adult and allow children to provide illustrations.

- Have a "Share Your Favorite Book" day.

- Have a "Dress as Your Favorite Book Character" day.

- Participate in group story-telling. Place magazine pictures in plastic eggs. During story time, let one child choose an egg, open it, and start a story about the picture. Have each child add a sentence or two to the story as you go around the circle.

- Invite a children's librarian or the owner of a children's book store to visit and share his or her favorite book.

- Decorate walls with posters from the American Library Association.

- Introduce children to a variety of literature characters through first-person role-playing.

- Together, check out a book from your classroom library. Mark its "due date" on the calendar. When the due date arrives, return the book to the classroom library and repeat the procedure.

117

Dear Parents:

We are preparing a Little Folks' Library Theme Center in our classroom during these dates: _____. This center will provide an opportunity for the children to participate in dramatic play and will serve as a basis for classroom discussion and learning activities. Below you will find a list of items that we need to furnish the center:

☐ Small flashlight   ☐ Individual student picture

☐ Index cards   ☐ Paint sticks

☐ Date stamp   ☐ Floor pillows

☐ Stamp pad   ☐ Magazines

☐ Rubber stamps   ☐ _____

Please return the items checked above by _____.

You can support the use of this center by talking to your child about the theme, planning family excursions related to the theme, or by sharing books that will provide your child with more information. A suggested literature list is available upon request.

Parent Name _____

Phone Number _____ ☐ I would love to help!

118

Preschool Office

A DECADE OF SALES

7,000
6,000
5,000
4,000
3,000
2,000
1,000

'87 '88 '89 '90 '9_ '9_ '96

1	2	3	4
7		9	10
11	12	13	14
17	18	19	20

MAY 1-5

	MON	TUES	WED	THURS	FRI
9:00					
10:00					
11:00					
12:00					
1:00					
2:00					
3:00					
4:00					

Theme Centers for Dramatic Play

Center Set-Up

Floorplan

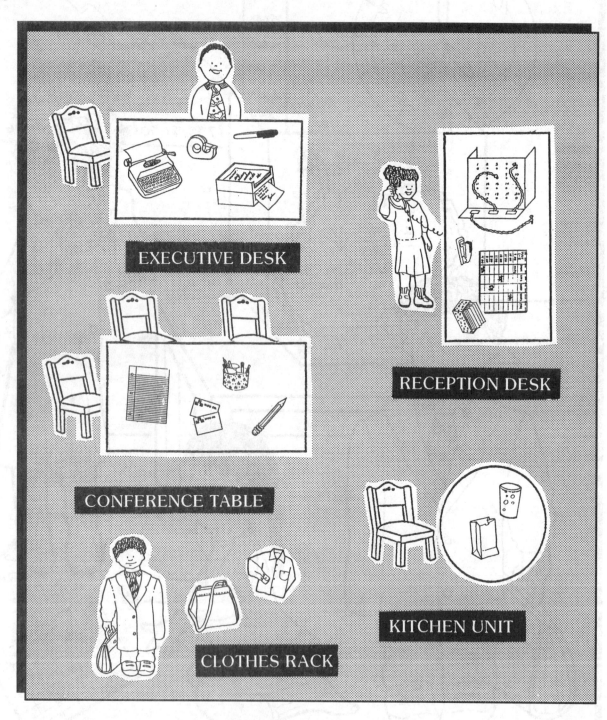

EXECUTIVE DESK

RECEPTION DESK

CONFERENCE TABLE

KITCHEN UNIT

CLOTHES RACK

CENTER SET-UP

☀ FURNISHINGS AND ACCESSORIES

Executive Desk
- Telephone
- "In" & "Out" boxes
- Blotter
- Typewriter & paper
- Keyboard from computer
- Cellophane tape dispenser

Supply Closet
- Hole punches (regular & decorative)
- Large paper clips
- Brads
- Ties
- Paper scraps

Conference Table
- Pencil sharpener
- Cup of unsharpened pencils
- Business Cards (Props to Make)

Clothes Rack
- Dresses
- Dress shirts
- Ties
- Belts
- Shoes
- Suit coats
- Business hats
- Purses

Reception Desk
- PBX Board and phone (Bare-Budget Furnishings)
- Stapler
- Card File (Props to Make)
- Appointment Book (Props to Make)

Kitchen Unit
- Coffee cups
- Plastic sponges
- Plastic donuts & cookies
- Water bottle
- Lunch bags

121

Center Set-Up

Bare-Budget Furnishings

PBX Phone Panel

Materials
- Cardboard box
- Golf tees
- Markers
- Ice pick
- Scissors
- Yarn
- Duct tape

Directions
1. Cut away one side of box and open as in diagram.
2. Use the ice pick to punch holes in the box as shown.
3. Use markers to make numbers.
4. To make phone cords, tape lengths of yarn to flap of box. Attach golf tees to the ends of the yarn strands.

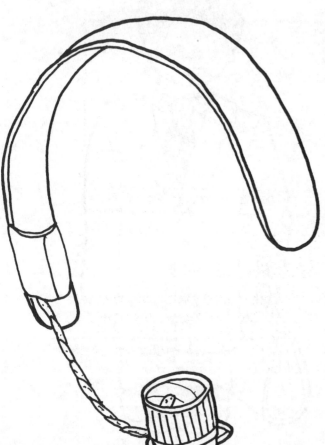

PBX Phone Panel Headset

Materials
- Scissors
- Plastic headband
- 2 pipe cleaners
- Catsup bottle lid
- Duct tape

Directions
1. Twist pipe cleaners together.
2. Open lid and slide pipe cleaners inside. Secure by closing lid tightly.
3. Wrap pipe cleaner and lid with duct tape.
4. Tape to headband.

Theme Centers for Dramatic Play

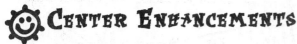

CENTER SET-UP

CENTER ENHANCEMENTS

Office Windows

Paint "skyscraper" style windows on butcher paper and attach to the wall in the executive office.

Sales Chart

On tagboard, use markers to create a colorful sales chart that graphs the rise and fall of sales. Display in the "conference room."

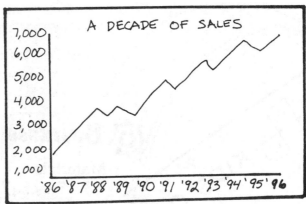

A DECADE OF SALES

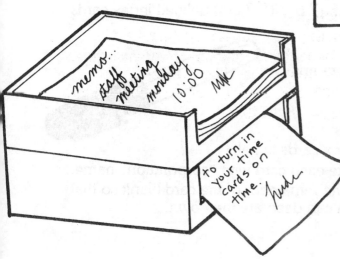

"In" & "Out" Boxes

Stack similar-sized gift boxes to create "In" and "Out" boxes. Cut out a rectangle at one end for easy access. Tape boxes together and cover or paint as desired.

PROPS TO MAKE

☀ APPOINTMENT BOOK

Materials
- 12 x 18-inch (30.5 x 45.7 cm) piece of cardboard
- Several pieces of construction paper, 12 x 18 inches (30.5 x 45.7 cm)
- Stapler
- Ruler
- Marker

Directions
1. Staple the sheets of construction paper to the cardboard securely.
2. Using ruler and marker, create the headings for an appointment book.

☀ BUSINESS CARDS

Materials
- 3 x 5-inch (7.6 x 12.7 cm) unlined index cards
- Scissors
- Markers
- Rubber stamps
- Stamp pads

Directions
1. Cut index cards in half.
2. Decorate each card with "corporation" name.
3. Leave the remainder of the card blank so that children can decorate their own.

124

PROPS TO MAKE

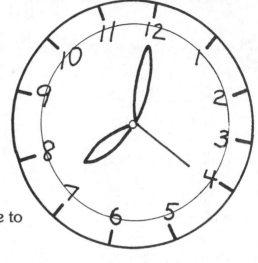

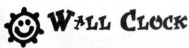

WALL CLOCK

Materials
- Sturdy 8-inch (20 cm) paper plate
- Brass brad
- Tagboard
- Ice pick
- Scissors
- Markers

Directions
1. Use markers to print numbers on the paper plate to make the clock face.
2. Cut the hands of the clock from tagboard.
3. Use ice pick to punch holes in hands and clock face.
4. Attach hands to clock face with the brad.

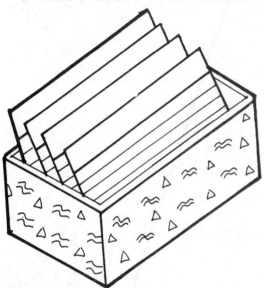

CARD FILE

Materials
- Empty   zip-lock bag box
- Construction paper
- White glue   • Scissors
- 5 x 8-inch (12.7 x 20.3 cm) index cards

Directions
1. Cut the side off of the box.
2. Cover with construction paper.
3. Add file cards.

TIE

Materials
- Tie pattern (following page)
- Tagboard
- Stapler
- Yarn
- Scissors

Directions
1. Use pattern to cut tie from tagboard.
2. Center tie on 2-foot (61 cm) length of yarn and staple in place.

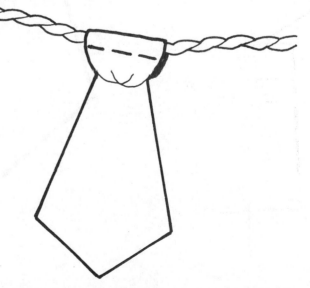

125

PROP PATTERN

126

Theme Centers for Dramatic Play

Teaching Tips

Center Tips

Introducing the Center
Arrive in class dressed as an executive carrying a briefcase. Have the briefcase filled with office items: stapler, daytimer, small phone, tape dispenser, pens. Ask children to identify items. Discuss their uses and where they are found. Direct children's attention to the center.

Safety Tips
- Caution children to press the brads away from their hands.
- Remind children that fingers stay out of staplers.
- Tell children to tie the neckties loosely.

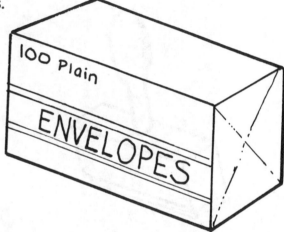

Center Variations

Office Supply Store
Add more stationery supplies and a cash register. Include receipt books and sales counters.

Public Service Office
Introduce information about police and fire stations, utilities offices and city hall. Visit a location or invite a representative to visit the class. Collect brochures and information about the services provided.

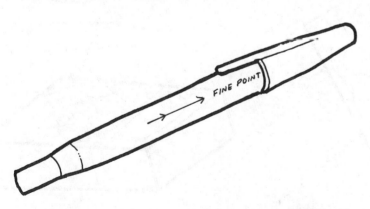

Developmental Activities

☼ Decorate a Necktie

Set out the blank neckties along with markers, collage materials (feathers, felt, buttons, rickrack) and glue. Invite children to create their own neckties.

Skills To Build
- Creating wih a variety of materials
- Experiencing the attributes of various materials

☼ Make a Business Card

Set out business cards that you have made. Put out markers, crayons, rubber stamps, pads and additional index cards. Let children create their own business cards and trade with classmates.

Skills To Build
- Building language skills
- Sharing

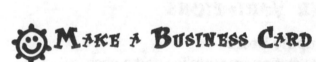

PAID

FIRST CLASS

FAXED

JUNE 12, 1997

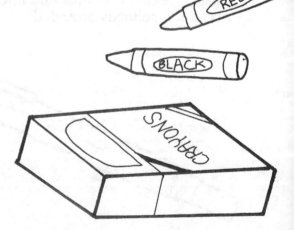

RED

BLACK

CRAYONS

128

Theme Centers for Dramatic Play

DEVELOPMENTAL ACTIVITIES

☼ PAPER CLIP SCULPTURE

Put out an assortment of paper clips (different sizes and colors). Attach several together and lay nearby. Let children create their own "sculptures."

Skills To Build
- Color identification
- Patterning
- Concept of length
- Size comparison

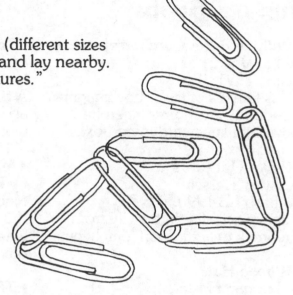

☼ HOLE PUNCH ART

Put out hole punches, both regular and decorative, along with construction paper and glue. Let children use their imagination to create art.

Skills To Build
- Small motor skills
- Acquiring skills with tools
- Creative expression

LITERATURE LIST

☀ PICTURE BOOKS

• *Willy and the Cardboard Boxes*
by Lizi Boyd;
Viking 1991. (PS)
In his father's office, a boy imagines wonderful adventures when he plays with large cardboard boxes.

• *Wake Up, City!*
by Alvin Tresselt;
Lothrop LB 1990. (PS-K)
Pictures activities in the city from daybreak until the work day begins.

• *Whose Hat?*
by Margaret Miller;
Greenwillow LB 1992. (PS-K)
A simple introduction to careers by showing hats such as a chef's hat and construction workers' hats.

• *Taxi: A Book of City Words*
by Betsy Maestro;
Houghton 1989. (PS-1)
A taxi picks up and drops off people all over the city. Along the way new words are introduced.

• *Mommy's Office*
by Barbara S. Hazen;
Macmillan LB 1992. (PS-1)
Emily spends an interesting day when her mother takes her to the office to show her how she works.

• *The Night Ones*
by Patricia Grossman;
Harcourt 1991. (PS-1)
The world of night workers is explored in text and drawings.

☀ BOOKS TO READ ALOUD

• *Night on Neighborhood Street*
by Eloise Greensfield;
Dial LB 19921. (K-3)
This picture book depicts life on the street of an inner-city neighborhood.

• *You're My Nikki*
by Phyllis R. Eisenberg;
Dial 1992. (PS-1)
Nikki is afraid that her single-parent mother will forget her when she starts her new job.

• *Jamal's Busy Day*
by Wade Hudson;
Just Us 1991. (PS-1)
Jamal prepares with his parents for a busy day—he will spend his at school and they at work.

• *Jeremy's Decision*
by Ardyth Broot;
Kane-Miller 1990. (PS-2)
Jeremy loves his father, a symphony orchestra conductor, but wants to become a paleographer.

• *Busy People*
by Nick Butterworth;
Candlewick 1992. (1-4)
Many community helpers are introduced in a question-and-answer format.

• *While You Are Asleep*
by Gwynne L. Isaacs;
Walker LB 1991. (PS-2)
This picture book describes the intersecting lives of several people who work at night.

130

Resources & More

Resources & Related Activities

- Assemble a variety of brads and set out in containers along with paper plates and construction paper scraps. Show the children how the brads work. Create an individual brad collage.

- Visit a local office.

- Invite a parent who works in an office to visit school.

- Visit an office supply store.

- Buy items at office store to use in class.

- Have a "Dress for the Office" day at school.

- Make a phone directory of all the offices where class parents work.

- Ask parents to send in business cards for children to share in class.

- Make a business card collage.

- Use tagboard to print each child's name and make a desk nameplate.

- Practice using play phones and role-play business conversations.

- Visit the school office and ask the secretary to share his or her duties.

- Practice communicating with a simple intercom.

- Brainstorm a list of buildings, other than an office, where people work.

131

Dear Parents:

   We are preparing a Kid's Corporation Theme Center in our classroom during these dates: _____. This center will provide an opportunity for the children to participate in dramatic play and will serve as a basis for classroom discussion and learning activities. Below you will find a list of items that we need to furnish the center:

☐ Stapler   ☐ Neckties

☐ Tape & dispenser   ☐ Brads

☐ Typing paper   ☐ Golf tees

☐ Old keyboard   ☐ Pencil sharpener

☐ Index cards   ☐ _____

   Please return the items checked above by _____.

   You can support the use of this center by talking to your child about the theme, planning family excursions related to the theme, or by sharing books that will provide your child with more information. A suggested literature list is available upon request.

Parent Name _____

Phone Number _____   ☐ I would love to help!

132

FIX-IT SHOP

Edupress   Theme Centers for Dramatic Play

CENTER SET-UP

🙂 FLOORPLAN

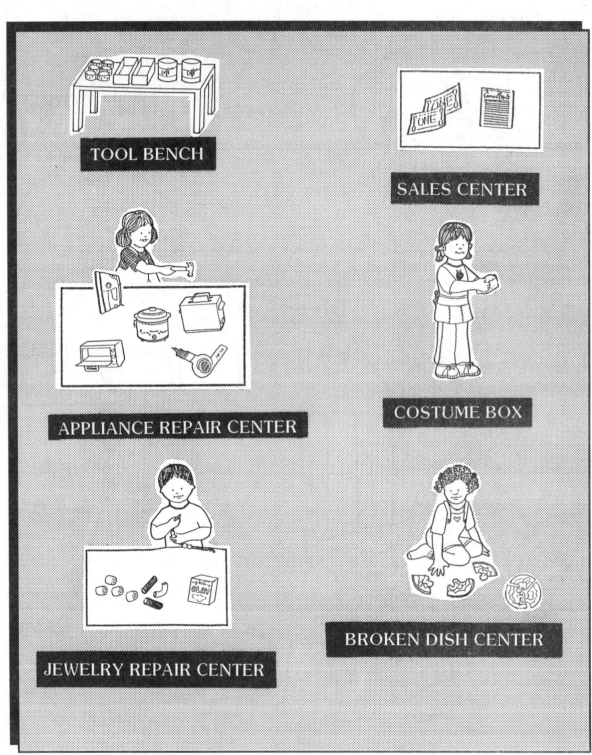

TOOL BENCH

SALES CENTER

APPLIANCE REPAIR CENTER

COSTUME BOX

JEWELRY REPAIR CENTER

BROKEN DISH CENTER

134

Furnishings and Accessories

Tool Bench
- Small tools (screwdriver, rubber-topped hammer, etc.)
- Hammering Board (Props to Make)
- Magnifying glasses
- Small flashlights
- Miscellaneous:
  rubber bands, toothpicks, string, tape, clothespins, paper clips, yarn, blunt needles, chopsticks, film canisters, magnets

Sales Center
- Sales receipt book
- Pencils, pencil holder
- Play money
- Cash register

Handyperson's Bookshelf
- How-to books
- Housewares catalogs
- Small appliance and toy assembly manuals
- Match-It Game Cards (Props to Make)

Handyperson's Costume Box
- Aprons
- Large shirts, pants, belts
- Eye glasses (no lenses)
- Tool Belt (page 292)
- Pants

Appliance Repair Center
- Camera
- Transistor radio
- Clocks
- Small appliances, cord and plug removed
- Mini-Storage Bin (Props to Make)
- Assorted screws, blunt nails, nuts, bolts

Toy and Doll Repair Center
- Dolls, old toys, stuffed animals

Jewelry Repair Center
- Beads (Props to Make)
- Shoelaces, yarn, string cut in various lengths
- Costume jewelry beads (large enough for children to handle)

Broken Dish Center
- Broken Plates (Props to Make)

Finishing Touches Center
- Paint brushes
- Paint
- Sponges
- Newspaper
- Q-tips™
- Toothbrushes
- Polishing cloths
- Objects to paint and polish

135

Center Set-Up

Bare-Budget Furnishings

Tool Bench

Turn an ordinary table into a tool bench by adding lots of bins, and compartments (Props to Make). Use coffee cans, margarine tubs, shoeboxes, and plastic containers as places for sorting and storing a variety of "fix-it" tools (Center Set-Up).

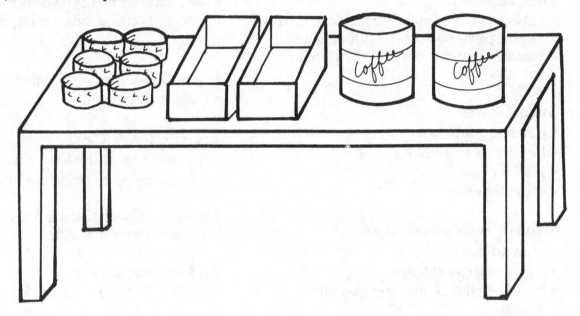

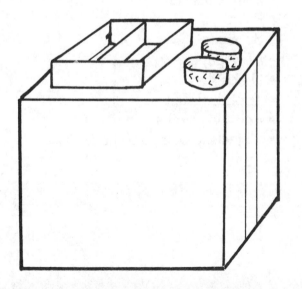

Apprentice Work Bench

Use hot glue to affix a drawer divider and other compartmentalized containers and boxes to the top of a cardboard box. Place at least one in each repair center area. Stock compartments with fix-it materials as indicated in Center Set-Up.

136

Theme Centers for Dramatic Play

Center Set-Up

☺ Center Enhancements

Ceiling Signs

Use actual objects to create ceiling signs that hang over each repair center.
- Hang bracelets, necklaces and other costume jewelry over the *Jewelry Repair Center.*
- Suspend a stuffed animal or toy plane over the *Toy Repair Center.*
- Dangle a colorful paper plate over the *Broken Dish Center.*
- Hang paper play money over the *Sales Center.*
- Suspend a paint brush over the *Finishing Touches Center.*
- Hang a book over the *Handyperson's Bookshelf.*
- Tie an egg beater blade to yarn to dangle over the *Appliance Repair Center.*

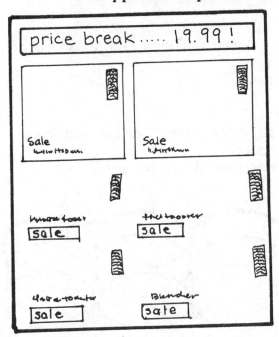

price break ..... 19.99 !

Sale

Sale

sale   sale

sale   Blender
sale

Match-It Game Wall

Decorate a portion of the center walls with newspaper and catalog advertisements for household items and small appliances. Post at eye-level. Put a strip of sticky-back Velcro™ next to the picture of each appliance.

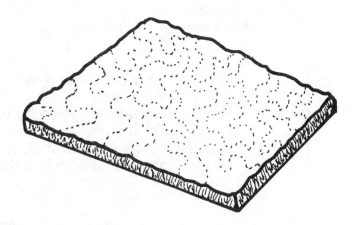

Rug Separators

Use carpet samples or small throw rugs to designate each small repair center. Place the Apprentice Tool Benches (Bare-Budget Furnishings) on the rugs.

PROPS TO MAKE

☀ BROKEN DISHES

Materials
- Paper plates in a variety of colors and party patterns—one per color or design
- Scissors

Directions
Cut each plate into two or more pieces, similar to a jigsaw puzzle.

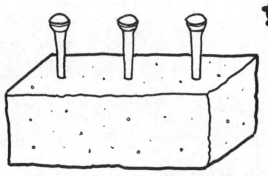

☀ HAMMERING PAD

Materials
- Thick (3 inches/7.6 cm or more) Styrofoam™ rectangle
- Golf tees

Directions
1. Partially insert several golf tees into the Styrofoam.™
2. Place additional tees in a small box.

☀ MINI STORAGE BIN

Materials
- Tuna cans (or other similar-sized cans)
- Masking tape
- Scissors
- Contact paper or gift wrap

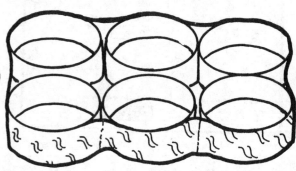

Directions
1. Place the tuna cans side-by-side to create two or more rows of cans.
2. Use masking tape around the perimeter of all the cans to hold them together.
3. Cut and adhere contact or other colorful paper to fit the height and perimeter of the bin.

Theme Centers for Dramatic Play

PROPS TO MAKE

☼ STRINGING BEADS

Materials
- Self-hardening clay
- Small dowel or unsharpened pencil
- 1 cup (250 ml) tube pasta
- Food coloring (5-8 drops)
- 1 tsp. (5 ml) rubbing alcohol **or** white vinegar
- Plastic mixing bowl
- Spoon
- Paper towels

Directions
1. *Clay beads:* Roll small bits of clay in the palm of the hand to create round bead shapes. Use a small dowel or unsharpened pencil to poke a hole through the center.

2. *Pasta beads:* Mix rubbing alcohol and food coloring in the mixing bowl. Place pasta in mixture. When desired color is achieved, place pasta on paper towels to dry.

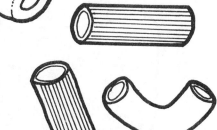

☼ MATCH-IT GAME CARDS

Materials
- Small appliance patterns, following
- Index cards
- Glue
- Scissors
- Crayons
- Sticky-back Velcro ™

Directions
1. Reproduce the pattern page several times.
2. Color the pictures.
3. Cut out around the edges.
4. Glue each picture to an index card.
5. Tape one half of sticky-back Velcro™ to the back of each card.

Theme Centers for Dramatic Play

Prop Pattern

Theme Centers for Dramatic Play

TEACHING TIPS

☺ CENTER TIPS

Introducing the Center

A day prior to introducing the center, invite each child to bring in a favorite small doll, stuffed animal, or toy to share. Talk about how they might feel if this special belonging were broken or missing parts. Introduce the concept of repair. Using the belongings as examples, share what might be broken and how it could be fixed. Encourage the children to join in creating solutions.

Safety Tips

- Demonstrate the proper way to hold and use the small tools.
- Beads are for stringing, not placing in the mouth!
- Explain the importance of returning all items to their storage compartments. So many small items can create a hazard if left on the floor.

☺ CENTER VARIATIONS

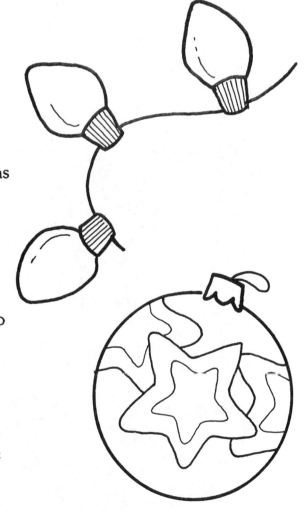

Santa's Workshop

- Turn the center into an elves' workshop during the holidays. Simply add Christmas decorations to enhance the center environment.
- Add small stools, just right for hard-working elves.
- Involve children in making holiday wish-lists for the elves.
- Add holiday clothing, slippers, hats, and Mr. and Mrs. Claus outfits (if available) to the costume box.

Yard Sale

- Remove Apprentice Tool Benches and replace them with higher tables.
- Put up signs announcing a yard sale.
- Sell the items created and repaired in the Fix-It stage of the center.

141

DEVELOPMENTAL ACTIVITIES

MATCH-IT GAME

Play a game with the Handyperson's Wall (Center Enhancements) and Match-It Game Cards (Props to Make). Select a game card and match it to a picture on the wall. Attach the card to the wall by aligning the Velcro™.

Skills To Build
• Object identification
• Matching
• Visual discrimination

DISH PUZZLERS

"Repair" Broken Dishes (Props to Make) by finding the matching plate pieces and putting them together like a jigsaw puzzle to create a whole plate.

Skills To Build
• Patterns
• Matching
• Visual discrimination
• Small motor
• Identifying similarities and differences

142

Theme Centers for Dramatic Play

DEVELOPMENTAL ACTIVITIES

☺ HAMMER BAMMERS

Choose golf tees to insert into Hammering Pad (Props to Make) and gently hammer them in. Try creating color patterns or shapes with the position of the tees.

Skills To Build
- Color identification
- Patterning
- Eye-hand coordination

☺ JEWELRY STRING UP

Use shoelaces, yarn, or string to create colorful costume jewelry.

Skills To Build
- Eye-hand coordination
- Counting
- Color and pattern identificaiton
- Visual discrimination
- Sequencing

143

LITERATURE LIST

PICTURE BOOKS

• **Who Uses This?**
by Margaret Miller;
Greenwillow LB 1990. (PS-K)
The uses of tools such as the
hammer and scissors are pictured.

• **Tools**
by Ann Morris;
Lothrop LB 1992. (PS-2)
A description of the functions of
various tools, aided by color photos.

• **A Carpenter**
by Douglas Florian;
Greenwillow LB 1991. (PS-K)
The work of a craftsman is
introduced with handsome
simplicity.

• **Maybe a Band-Aid Will Help**
by Anna Grossnickle Hines;
Dutton 1984.(PS-1)
Sarah tries to repair her broken doll.

• **Mr. Bear's Chair**
by Thomas Graham;
Dutton 1990. (PS-1)
When Mrs. Bear's chair breaks, Mr.
Bear says he'll build a new one.

• **At Taylor's Place**
by Sharon P. Denslow;
Macmillan 1990. (K-2)
Tory visits Taylor's workshop,
where he has just completed carving
a weather vane.

BOOKS TO READ ALOUD

• **No Problem**
by Eileen Browne;
Simon & Schuster 1991. (PS-3)
When Mouse receives a
construction kit, all her friends have
a try putting it together.

• **Tool Book**
by Gail Gibbons;
Holiday LB 1982. (K-3)
An introduction to various simple
tools and their uses.

• **The Man Who Was Too Lazy to
Fix Things**
by Phyllis Krasilovsky;
Morrow LB 1992. (PS-3)
A lazy man avoids home repair until
he gets the help of some relatives on
his birthday.

• **Fix It**
by David McPhail;
Dutton 1984. (PS-K)
Emma Bear is distraught when the
television set won't work.

• **Annie & Co.**
by David McPhail;
Henry Holt LB 1991. (PS-3)
Six-year-old Annie, who has
learned from her father, decides to
go out in the world and fix things.

• **Good As New**
by Barbara Douglass;
Lothrop LB 1982. (PS-2)
Grandfather restores Grady's
damaged teddy bear.

Resources & More

☺ Resources & Related Activities

- Take apart and examine things with magnifying glasses to discover "what's inside?"
  - a stuffed animal
  - a battery-operated flashlight
  - a watch
  - a camera
  - a radio

- Explore the concept of opposites using "fix-it" terms. Invite the children to find examples.
  - broken, fixed
  - old, new
  - shiny, dull
  - battery-operated, electrical

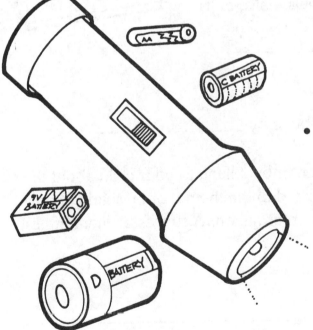

- Spend some time in the classroom looking for things that need repair. Make a list and send a copy home with each child requesting a parent to come in and do the repair. Schedule time for those who respond. Ask the children to carefully observe and ask questions during each "fix-it" event.

- Make some scientific discoveries:
  - Find out what happens to a flashlight, radio, toy or other battery-operated object with and without the batteries.
  - Compare different battery sizes.
  - Examine an electrical cord and plug. What happens to small appliances when they are plugged in? Talk about safety issues regarding wall sockets .
  - Use magnets to pick up small items from the Fix-It Center. Which ones have magnetic qualities?

- Locate businesses in the area that do repair. Arrange a visit to one. Take something in that needs repair and watch while you wait! Some suggestions: shoe repair, watch repair, vacuum cleaner repair.

- Visit a sporting goods store. Watch a bike being assembled.

145

Dear Parents:

We are preparing a Fix-It Shop Theme Center in our classroom during these dates: _____. This center will provide an opportunity for the children to participate in dramatic play and will serve as a basis for classroom discussion and learning activities. Below you will find a list of items that we need to furnish the center:

☐ Small hammer ☐ Screwdriver

☐ Broken appliance ☐ Doll

☐ Camera ☐ Stuffed animal

☐ Clock ☐ Screws, nails, bolts

☐ Flashlight ☐ _____

Please return the items checked above by _____.

You can support the use of this center by talking to your child about the theme, planning family excursions related to the theme, or by sharing books that will provide your child with more information. A suggested literature list is available upon request.

Parent Name _____

Phone Number _____ ☐ I would love to help!

146

Baby's Playpen

Theme Centers for Dramatic Play

Center Set-Up

Floorplan

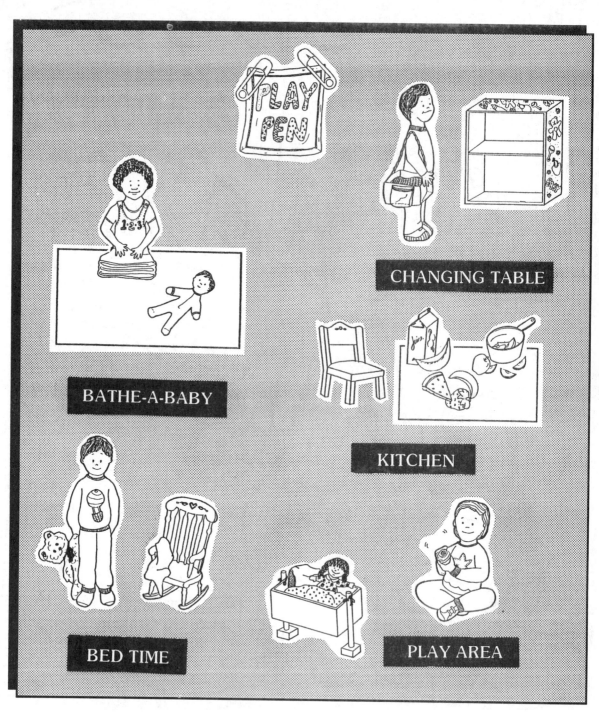

148

Theme Centers for Dramatic Play

CENTER SET-UP

☼ FURNISHINGS AND ACCESSORIES

Miscellaneous
- Baby dolls of realistic size and various ethnicities
- Stroller

Kitchen
- High chair
- Bibs
- Baby food jars
- Bottles
- Baby spoons and dishes

Bathe-A-Baby Area
- Bathing tub
- Sponges & washcloths
- Towels
- Baby dolls

Changing Table
- Diapers
- Baby clothes
- Changing Table (Bare-Budget Furnishings)
- Diaper Bags (Props to Make)

Play Area
- Rattle (Props to Make)
- Play pen
- Blocks
- Art supplies
- Rug
- Floor pillows

Bed Time
- Baby blankets
- Rocking chairs
- Baby's Bookshelf (Center-made picture books plus other related literature)
- Baby Cradle (Bare-Budget Furnishings)

149

Bare-Budget Furnishings

Changing Table
Materials
- 2 cardboard boxes
- Wide masking tape
- Baby-design gift wrap

Directions
1. Cut open one side of each box.
2. Stack one box on top of the other, open sides facing the same direction.
3. Tape the boxes together securely.
4. Cover with baby-design gift wrap.

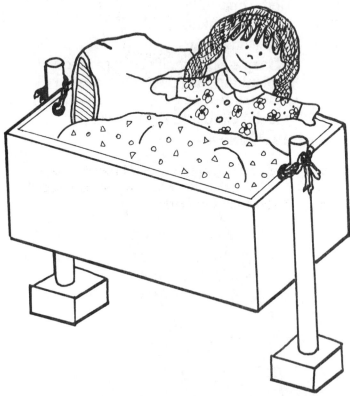

Baby Cradle
Materials
- 2 pieces of wood approximately 8 x 4 x 2 inches (20 x 10 x 5 cm)
- Cardboard box
- Two 3-foot (1 m) dowels or PVC pipe
- String

Directions
1. Drill a hole the diameter of the dowel or pipe in the center of the wood supports.
2. Insert the dowel in the hole.
3. Cut a hole in each end of cardboard box.
4. Thread the string through each hole and tie securely to the dowels. The cradle should rock.

☼ CENTER ENHANCEMENTS

Center Sign

Cut and glue cloth or paper letters over a baby blanket to create a sign naming the center. "Hang" the sign with oversized safety pins cut from pastel-colored butcher paper.

Rocking Chair

Locate a real rocking chair to place in the center. Position it on a throw rug to keep it from sliding on the floor.

PROPS TO MAKE

☀ BABY CARRIER

Materials
- Fabric
- Yarn
- Cloth tape

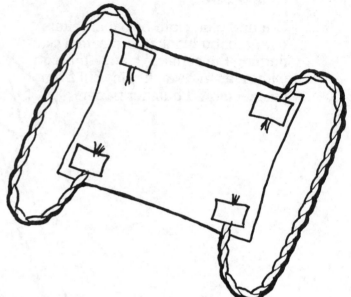

Directions
1. Cut material into 12 x 18-inch (30.5 x 45.7 cm) rectangle.
2. Cut yarn into two 18-inch (30.5 cm) lengths.
3. Tape yarn, as shown, to cloth rectangle.

☀ BABY RATTLES

Materials
- Egg cartons
- Scissors
- Dried beans or rice
- Masking tape

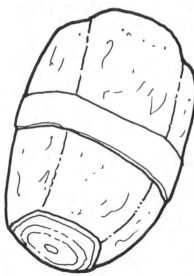

Directions
1. Partially fill an egg carton cup with dried beans or rice.
2. Invert a second cup over the opening of the first.
3. Tape closed securely with masking tape.

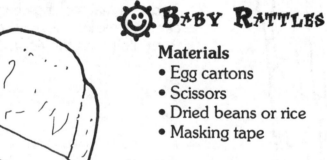

152

Theme Centers for Dramatic Play

Props to Make

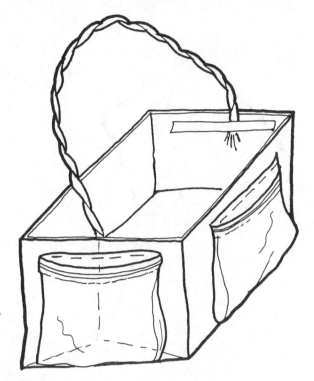

☀ Diaper Bag

Materials
- Brown shopping bag
- 4 zip-top plastic bags
- Stapler   • Scissors
- Yarn   • Masking tape

Directions
1. Cut the shopping bag in half. Open.
2. Open the zip-top bags and securely staple one to each side of the bag. Cover the staples on the inside of the bag with masking tape to hold in place.
3. Staple a yarn handle to the top of the bag. Secure with masking tape.

☀ Baby Bib

Material
- Pattern, following page
- Fabric
- Scissors
- Two 12-inch (30.5 cm) lengths of yarn or ribbon
- Needle and thread
- Straight pins

Directions
1. Cut out pattern.
2. Lay pattern on fabric. Pin in place.
3. Cut around pattern and remove pins.
4. Stitch yarn or ribbon to the fabric as indicated on the pattern.

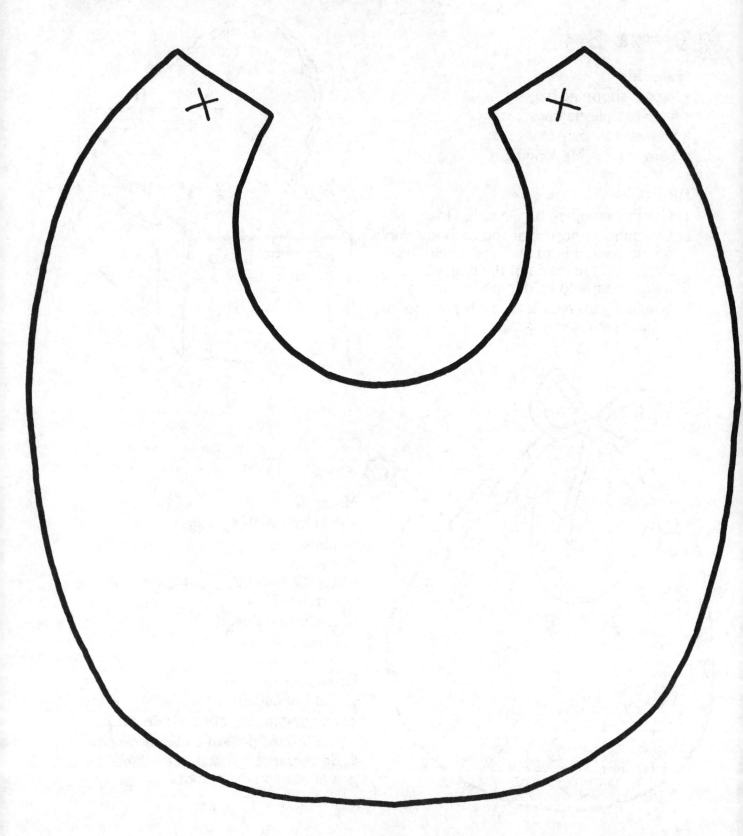

154

Teaching Tips

☼ Center Tips

Introducing the Center
Invite children to bring photographs of younger siblings. Share the photos during group or circle time. Exchange stories about ways they help with their younger brothers and sisters.

Safety Tips
- Practice rocking in the rocking chair. Caution children against rocking too hard.
- Demonstrate how to rock the cradle. Explain that if they push too hard someone will be hit by the box.

☼ Center Variations

Pet Care Center
Replace the baby dolls with stuffed animals. Exchange baby accessories with leashes, pet combs, eating bowls and play toys.

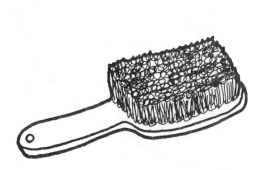

Developmental Activities

Rhythm Rattles

Shake, rattle and roll a variety of rattles in time to music.

Skills To Build
- Listening
- Small motor skills
- Patterning
- Rhythm

Fold and Stack

Fold and stack diapers and baby blankets into different sized shapes and stacks. Count the number of diapers in a stack.

Skills To Build
- Shape identification
- Small motor skills
- Counting

156

DEVELOPMENTAL ACTIVITIES

BABY BOOKS

Cut and paste pictures to folded
construction paper books. "Read"
bedtime stories to the babies.

Skills To Build
• Creative thinking
• Sequencing

PACK A DIAPER BAG

Get baby ready to go out by packing a
diaper bag with everything you'll need.

Skills To Build
• Size discrimination
• Spatial awareness
• Small motor skills

© Edupress   *Theme Centers for Dramatic Play*

LITERATURE LIST

PICTURE BOOKS

• **The Book of Babies**
by Jo Foord, illus.;
Random 1991. (PS)
A celebration of the activities of
early childhood.

• **Say Goodnight**
by Helen Oxenbury;
Macmillan 1987. (PS)
A group of babies engage in
goodnight activities.

• **Rolling Rose**
by James Stevenson;
Greenwillow 1992. (PS)
No one pays attention to baby Rose
in her rolling walker, so she just rolls
out the door for adventure.

• **Where's the Baby?**
by Pat Hutchins;
Greenwillow LB 1988.(PS-K)
Hazel despairs of the mess her baby
brother makes in the house.

• **Bye Bye Baby: A Sad Story
With A Happy Ending**
by Janet & Allan Ahlberg;
Little 1990. (PS-1)
A baby, who has no family and lives
alone, sets out to find himself a
home.

• **Bear and Mrs. Duck**
by Elizabeth Winthrop;
Holiday LB 1988. (PS-K)
Mrs. Duck comes to bear-sit when
Teddy Bear has the sniffles.

BOOKS TO READ ALOUD

• **The Gigantic Baby**
by Mordicai Gerstein;
Harper LB 1991. (PS-3)
A baby grows to such gigantic
proportions that a telescope is
needed to examine her ears.

• **My New Baby-Sitter**
by Christine Loomis;
Morrow LB 1991. (PS-2)
About baby-sitters: how to choose
them, what they do and questions
children have about them.

• **Eleanor and the Babysitter**
by Susan Hellard;
Little 1991. (PS-3)
Eleanor resents her new baby-sitter
until the baby-sitter saves her from a
monster.

• **More Bunny Trouble**
by Hans Wilhelm;
Scholastic 1989. (PS-1)
Ralph is tapped to babysit his bunny
sister, but he lets her get out of sight
and lost.

• **The Snow Lady**
by Shirley Hughes;
Lothrop LB 1990. (K-3)
Sam regrets the unkindness she and
her brother show their baby-sitter.

• **What Kind of Baby-Sitter Is
This?**
by Dolores Johnson;
Macmillan 1991. (PS-2)
Kevin is surprised when he finds his
new baby-sitter, an elderly lady,
loves baseball.

RESOURCES & MORE

RESOURCES & RELATED ACTIVITIES

- Listen to and learn some lullabies to sing.

- Play a rattle game. Give each child a rattle. Shake a rhythm. Children try to repeat the rhythm.

- Cook peeled and chopped apples in water until soft. Puree in a blender and enjoy some applesauce.

- Develop listening skills by imitating the different sounds made by a crying baby.

- Pair up to use a baby blanket in a motor development game. Place lightweight foam balls in the center of a baby blanket. With a child on opposite sides, pick up the blanket edges and toss the balls into the air, trying to catch them before they touch the ground.

- Visit a local hospital (with permission) and view the newborn babies through the visitors window.

- Use funnels to fill baby bottles with water, then screw on the nipple and cap. Talk about the concept of suction and drink through a straw.

- Have crawling races.

Dear Parents:

We are preparing a Baby Care Theme Center in our classroom during these dates: _____. This center will provide an opportunity for the children to participate in dramatic play and will serve as a basis for classroom discussion and learning activities. Below you will find a list of items that we need to furnish the center:

☐ Stroller   ☐ Empty baby food jars

☐ Baby blankets   ☐ Rocking chair

☐ High chair   ☐ Diapers

☐ Baby dolls   ☐ Bathing tub

☐ Baby toys   ☐ _____

Please return the items checked above by _____.

You can support the use of this center by talking to your child about the theme, planning family excursions related to the theme, or by sharing books that will provide your child with more information. A suggested literature list is available upon request.

Parent Name _____

Phone Number _____ ☐ I would love to help!

Keeping House

Edupress   *Theme Centers for Dramatic Play*

CENTER SET-UP

Floorplan

COSTUME BOX

LAUNDRY CENTER

KITCHEN UNIT

CLEANING CORNER

EATING NOOK

162

FURNISHINGS AND ACCESSORIES

Kitchen Unit
- Dishpans
- Recipe box w/Cards (Props to Make)
- Plastic dishes
- Nylon scrubbies
- Dishwashing liquid
- Dish drainer
- Cookbooks

Laundry Center
- Washer-Dryer (Bare-Budget Furnishings)
- Drying Rack (page 206)
- Laundry baskets
- Sorting table
- Clothing
- Clothespins
- Clothesline
- Socks, assorted colors
- Assorted towels
- Laundry Soap (Props to Make)
- Measuring cups
- Small tubs
- Ironing board
- Iron

Costume Box
- Aprons
- Rubber gloves
- Shirts
- Shorts
- Pants

Eating Nook
- Plastic dishes, knives, forks, spoons
- Placemats
- Napkins
- Silverware bin (Props to Make)

Cleaning Corner
- Cleaning supply shelf
- Cleaning Caddy (Center Enhancements)
- Spray bottles filled with water
- Feather Duster (Props to Make)
- Broom & dust pan
- Mop

163

Center Set-Up

Bare-Budget Furnishings

Washer-Dryer
Materials
- 2 square cardboard boxes
- Duct tape
- Tempera paint

Directions
1. Stack boxes and tape together.
2. Paint a round "window" on the front of each box.
3. Cut three sides of the front flap of each box so that door lifts up.

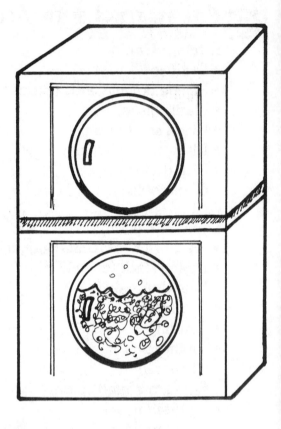

Clothesline
Materials
- 2 pieces PVC pipe, 3 feet (1 m) long
- 2 large coffee cans
- Sand
- Clothesline

Directions
1. Fill coffee cans with sand and stand one piece of PVC pipe in each.
2. Tie clothesline securely between the pipes.

164

Center Set-Up

Center Enhancements

Laundry Baskets

Add two plastic laundry baskets (or make them from boxes) filled with clothes for sorting by color and type.

Cleaning Caddy

Cover outside of a compartmentalized soft drink carrier with contact paper. Use to store and carry cleaning supplies.

Magnet Wall

Use double-stick velcro® to attach cookie sheets to the center wall at child level. Keep a supply of refrigerator magnets in a box nearby for creating pictures, identifying objects and simple story-telling

Props to Make

Laundry Soap

Materials
- Empty detergent box with fliptop
- Cornmeal

Directions
Fill the detergent box with cornmeal.

Feather Duster

Materials
- Yarn
- Duct tape
- Wooden dowel, 12 inches (30.5 cm) long

Directions
1. Wrap yarn around a magazine 35-40 times.
2. Using another strand of yarn, tie the loops together at one end of the magazine, knotting tightly.
3. Cut the loops at the other end of the bundle.
4. Wrap the ends of the tying strand around the end of the dowel and tape securely.

166

PROPS TO MAKE

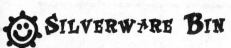 **SILVERWARE BIN**

Materials
- Shirt-sized gift box
- Contact paper or gift wrap
- Scissors
- Clear tape

Directions
1. Cover lid and bottom of box with contact paper or gift wrap.
2. Cut the box lid into two strips the height and length of the box bottom.
3. Tape the strips into the box bottom to create three dividers.

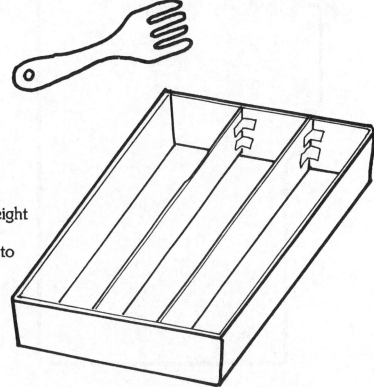

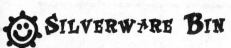 **RECIPE CARDS**

Materials
- Recipe card pattern, following
- Magazines with food pictures
- Card stock
- Scissors
- Glue

Directions
1. Reproduce recipe card pattern onto card stock.
2. Cut food pictures from magazines and glue to cards.

167

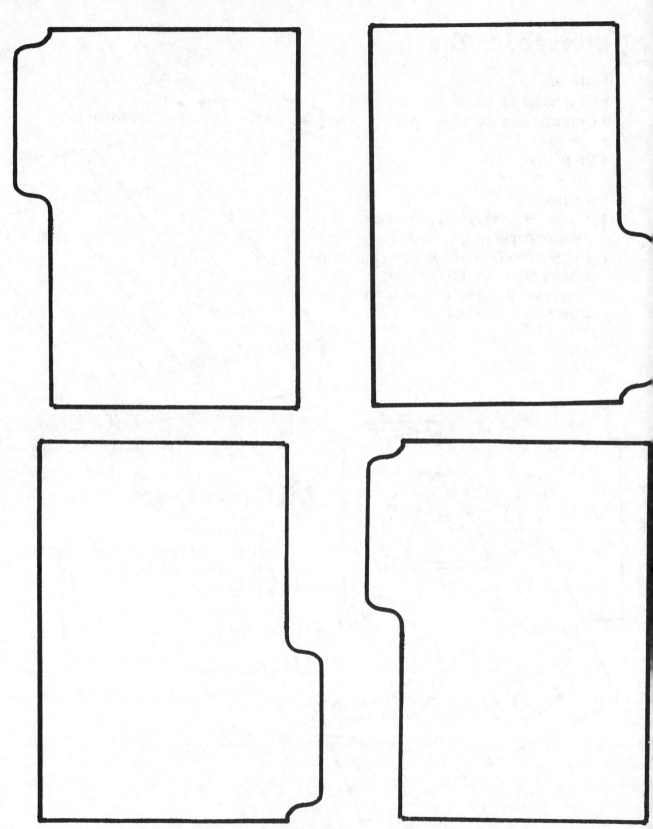

168

TEACHING TIPS

☺ CENTER TIPS

Introducing the Center
Fill a tub with cleaning items such as: sponge, dustpan, bar of soap, feather duster. Pull the items, one at a time, out of the box and invite children to identify each one and tell how it might be used.

Safety Tips
- Discuss the fact that cleaning items used in the center are either pretend or harmless and that many at home could be dangerous.
- Caution children that soap burns when it gets in the eyes and tastes terrible on the tongue!
- Explain that feather dusters might feel good when brushed against one's skin, but should be kept away from the face, particularly the eyes.

☺ CENTER VARIATIONS

Alphabet Station
- Put letter magnets on the refrigerator wall.
- Sweep up construction paper letters into the dustpan.
- Spray water on a plastic plate then trace letters in the water.
- Put assorted colored letters on the recipe cards (Props to Make) and sort the cards by color and identical letters.
- Provide blank Post-It™ note pads and crayons. Encourage children to write letters on them and decorate the center.

"Around the House" Art Studio
- Put tempera paint into pie tins and make prints from housekeeping objects such as a hand egg-beater, paper cups, plastic forks, sponges, nylon scrubbies, bottle caps from plastic bottles.
- Put tempera paint in liquid soap dispensers and squirt some simple designs on construction paper.
- Wear rubber gloves and fingerpaint on large sheets of newsprint. Display the dried paintings on the center wall.
- Paint with a mixture of liquid soap and food coloring for some unusual results.

169

Developmental Activities

Laundry Time

Leave an assortment of towels and clothing in laundry basket for sorting, folding, and hanging with clothespins on the clothesline.

Skills To Build
- Small motor
- Color identification

Recipe Card Roundup

Use recipe cards for a variety of "tasty" activities: "create" meals; sort by food category; identify the picture.

Skills To Build
- Vocabulary building
- Categorizing
- Creative thinking

170

Developmental Activities

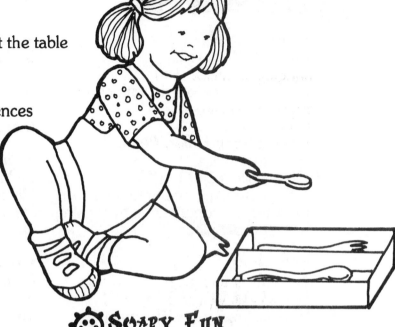

☺ Sort and Set

Sort silverware into the bin and set the table for meal times.

Skills To Build
- Identifying similarities and differences
- Sorting
- Concept of left and right

☺ Soapy Fun

Measure detergent and pour it in the bin for "washing" the laundry.

Skills To Build
- Measuring
- Eye-hand coordination
- Concept of volume
- Dry measurement

LITERATURE LIST

PICTURE BOOKS

• *Can I Help?*
by Anne Rockwell;
Macmillan 1982. (PS)
A little girl tries to help with chores
around the house.

• *Everything Has a Place*
by Patricia Lillie;
Greenwillow 1993. (PS)
An oversized picture book that
explores the concept that everything
has a proper place.

• *Clean It!*
by Henry Pluckrose;
Watts LB 1991. (PS-1)
Various ideas associated with
cleaning are explored with color
photos and simple text.

• *Joey Runs Away*
by Jack Kent;
Simon & Schuster paper 1989. (PS-3)
Joey the kangaroo runs away when his
mother tells him to clean up his room
(her pouch).

• *Clean Your Room, Harvey Moon!*
by Margery Cuyler;
Macmillan 1991. (PS-3)
Harvey's mother orders him to clean
up his room.

• *Tucker and the Bear*
by Jane Chambless;
Simon & Schuster 1989. (PS-2)
Tucker, who lives alone, reluctantly
agrees to share his quarters with a bear.

BOOKS TO READ ALOUD

• *Keeping House*
by Margaret Mahy;
Macmillan 1991. (PS-2)
When Lizzie hires a man to clean
her house, she is so ashamed of the
mess that she cleans it up herself.

• *A Clean House for Mole and
  Mouse*
by Harriet Zilfert;
Viking 1988. (1-3)
Mouse and Mole decide to clean
house.

• *Mooch the Messy*
by Marjorie Sharmat;
Harper LB 1976. (1-2)
Mooch the rat lives in his messy rat
hole, much to the disgust of his
father, who tries to reform him.

• *Matthew's Dream*
by Leo Lionni;
Knopf LB 1991. (K-3)
With imagination, Matthew can turn
his home into something stunning.

• *Titch*
by Pat Hutchins;
Macmillan 1971. (1-3)
Tidy Titch helps his siblings clean up
and soon has all their junk in his
own room.

• *The Day That Henry Cleaned
  His Room*
by Sarah Wilson;
Simon & Schuster 1990. (PS-3)
Henry's room is so messy that even
scientists come to investigate the
growth on his walls.

172

RESOURCES & MORE

RESOURCES & RELATED ACTIVITIES

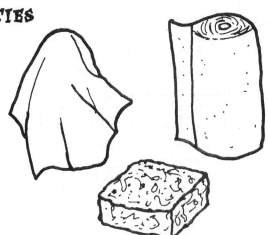

- Ask the local market to donate some cleaning products for your classroom center.

- Participate in tactile comparisons by gently rubbing these housekeeping related objects against the thigh or forearm:
  - scrub brush
  - washcloth
  - feather duster
  - paper towel
  - sponge
  - dust cloth
  - squeegee
  - rubber glove

- Sing a housekeeping song (to the tune of *Mulberry Bush*) and pantomime the actions:

  This is the way we wash our clothes,
  wash our clothes,
  wash our clothes.
  This is the way we wash our clothes,
  So early in the morning.

  Substitute these phrases:
  ...scrub the walls
  ...hang the clothes
  ...knead the bread
  ...dust the desk
  ...sweep the floor

  Invite the children to create their own descriptive phrases to sing.

- Develop large muscles and small motor skills with these "housekeeping" activities:
  - Sweep a ping-pong ball across the floor.
  - Crawl through a tunnel made from sheets.
  - Jump over a cushion left on the floor.
  - Pick up an object while wearing rubber gloves.
  - Squirt water from a paint sprayer into a cup.
  - Squeeze water out of a sponge.

173

Dear Parents:

We are preparing a Keeping House Theme Center in our classroom during these dates: _____. This center will provide an opportunity for the children to participate in dramatic play and will serve as a basis for classroom discussion and learning activities. Below you will find a list of items that we need to furnish the center:

☐ Clothespins   ☐ Rubber gloves

☐ Plastic utensils   ☐ Old socks

☐ Aprons   ☐ Old clothing

☐ Dish drainer   ☐ Broom

☐ Plastic dishes   ☐ _____

Please return items checked above by _____.

You can support the use of this center by talking to your child about the theme, planning family excursions related to the theme, or by sharing books that will provide your child with more information. A suggested literature list is available upon request.

Parent Name _____

Phone Number _____ ☐ I would love to help!

174

Flight of Fancy

Center Set-Up

Floorplan

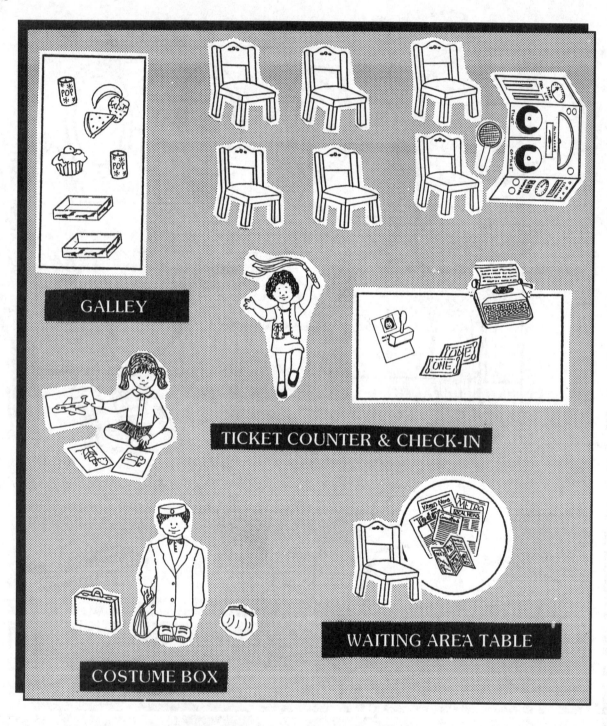

GALLEY

TICKET COUNTER & CHECK-IN

WAITING AREA TABLE

COSTUME BOX

176

CENTER SET-UP

☺ FURNISHINGS AND ACCESSORIES

Airplanes
- Control Panel (Bare-Budget Furnishings)
- Cabin Divider (Bare-Budget Furnishings)
- Radio Microphone (Props to Make)
- Pillows
- Blankets
- Magazines
- Maps
- Cards
- Small soaps
- Facial tissues

Waiting Area Table
- Magazines
- Travel brochures
- Maps

Costume Box
- Pilot's hat
- Other hats
- Coveralls
- Purses
- Dolls & clothes
- Briefcases
- Suit coats
- Diaper bags
- Suitcases
- Aprons

Airplane Galley
- Selection of dishes & foods
- Trays
- Empty soda cans & juice boxes
- Plastic divided plates
- Food Trays (Props to Make)

Ticket Counter & Check-In
- Hole punch
- Rubber stamps & pads
- Scale
- Cash register
- Typewriter
- Stapler
- Jet Stream Sticks (Props to Make)

177

CENTER SET-UP

BARE-BUDGET FURNISHINGS

Control Panel

Materials
- Large cardboard box
- Tempera paint
- Scissors
- Brass brads

Directions
1. Open seam of one side of the box and cut away one panel, leaving three.
2. Cut "window" in center panel. (This step is not necessary if a seated child can see over the box.)
3. On the plain side of the cardboard, decorate the panels with a series of dials and gauges. Examples: air speed, wind velocity, ground speed, altimeter, outside temperature fuel.
4. Use discarded panel to cut out two 12-inch (30.5 cm) circles.
5. Using brads, attach circles to control panel to simulate steering wheels.

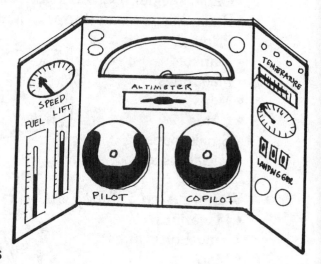

Cabin Divider

Materials
- 2 medium cardboard boxes
- 2 pieces tagboard
- Duct tape

Directions
1. Fold pieces of tagboard in half lengthwise.
2. Tape short sides together, leaving top open.
3. Use tape to attach to outside face of boxes.
4. Place boxes between passenger compartment chairs and flight deck, with pouch facing passengers. Place magazines and newspapers inside pouch, blankets and pillows inside box.

Theme Centers for Dramatic Play

CENTER SET-UP

☼ CENTER ENHANCEMENTS

Airplane Windows

Use butcher paper and paint the outlines of airplane windows. Cut out each window opening.

Airline Sign

Using tagboard or butcher paper and markers, create a wall sign that names the classroom airline.

Baggage Cart

Use a small metal wagon, block cart or baby carriage to simulate a baggage cart. Wrap butcher paper around the outside of the cart to camouflage it. Hang a "baggage" sign on the side.

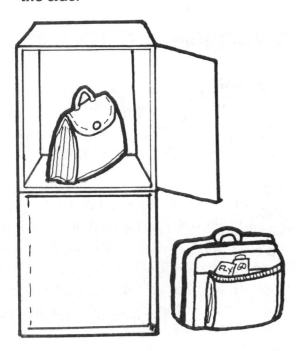

Storage Lockers

Use small cardboard boxes stacked one on top of the other to simulate lockers. Stack each box so that the opening faces the children. Leave one flap attached to be the locker door.

Props to Make

☺ Paper Airplanes

(Prop is appropriate for child participation)

Materials
- Airplane pattern (page 182)
- Paper
- Markers

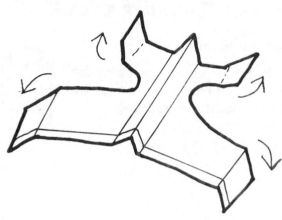

Directions
1. Duplicate airplane pattern onto paper.
2. Cut out and fold on dotted lines.
2. Decorate with markers.

☺ Flight Attendant Clipboard

Materials
- 10 x 12-inch (25 x 30 cm) piece of cardboard
- 24-inch (60 cm) length of string
- Scissors
- Tempera paint & brush
- 2 large paper clips
- Hole punch
- Pencil
- Tape

Directions:
1. Paint cardboard with tempera paint.
2. Punch a hole in the upper right hand corner of cardboard and tie string through hole.
3. Secure pencil to other end of string with tape.
4. Slide paper clips on the top of board and secure paper underneath them.

180

Theme Centers for Dramatic Play

Props to Make

Food Tray

(Prop is appropriate for child participation)
Materials
- Cardboard soda case
- Sponges cut in food or airplane shapes
- Tempera paint & brush
- Pie tins

Directions
1. Paint cardboard case and allow to dry.
2. Decorate with sponge shapes dipped in tempera paint.

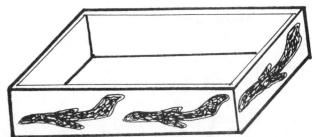

Radio Microphone

Materials
- Tongue depressor
- Construction paper
- Margarine tub lid
- Tacky glue
- Marker

Directions
1. Attach margarine lid to tongue depressor with tacky glue.
2. Cover both sides with a circle of paper the same size as the lid.
3. Decorate with marker.

Jet Stream Sticks

Materials
- Tongue depressor
- Crepe paper strips or curly ribbon
- Tape

Directions
1. Measure out several lengths of crepe paper or ribbon.
2. Attach to end of tongue depressor with tape. Store in coffee can until needed.

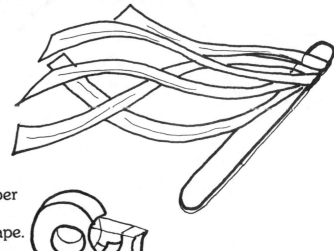

181

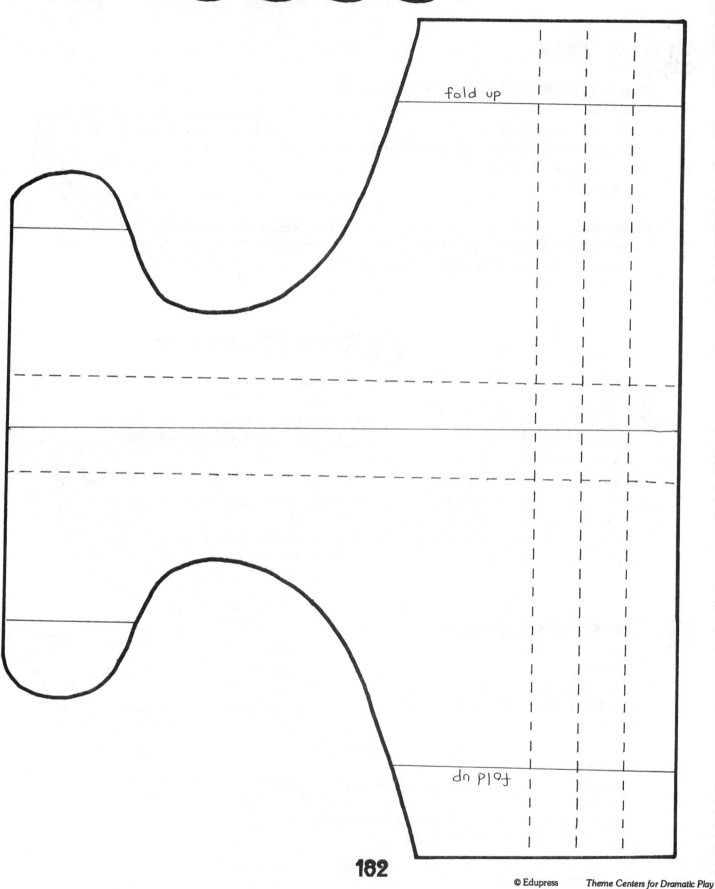

fold up

fold up

182

Theme Centers for Dramatic Play

☼ CENTER TIPS

Introducing the Center
During circle time, talk about flying in an airplane. Who has gone on an airplane? Where have they gone? Who did they visit? Use an audio tape and hand out Jet Stream Sticks (Props to Make). Role-play being an airplane in flight.

Safety Tips
• While "flying," don't crash into other airplanes.
• Remind the children that the instrument panel will fall over if it is leaned on.
• Remind the children that only two of them can fly the plane at one time, and that the plane only holds as many passengers as there are seats on board.

☼ CENTER VARIATIONS

Train
• Add tables to create a dining car.
• Include a train whistle in center.
• Stack nap mats or blankets on top of one another to simulate sleeping berths.
• Add large bandanas to costume box for engineers' kerchiefs.

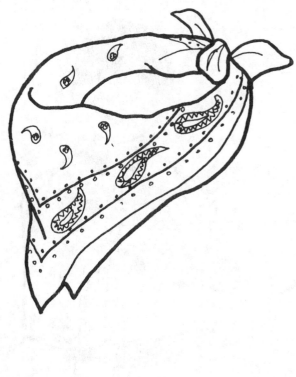

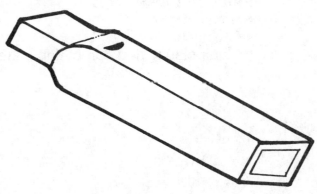

Theme Centers for Dramatic Play

DEVELOPMENTAL ACTIVITIES

FLYING

Play an audio tape that has a soaring quality to it. Have the children pretend they are flying and hold Jet Stream Sticks while they dance/fly.

Skills To Build
• Large motor—balance, dance skills
• Creative movement

MAP COLLAGE

Cut up pieces of maps from a variety of sources. Put in bin on art shelf. Have a variety of paper and glue available.

Skills To Build
• Small motor
• Creativity
• Manipulating and combining materials

Theme Centers for Dramatic Play

DEVELOPMENTAL ACTIVITIES

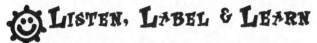

☺ LISTEN, LABEL & LEARN

Play an audio tape of a variety of sounds. Have
pictures that correspond to the sounds. Match the two.

Skills To Build
• Recognizing objects by sound and sight

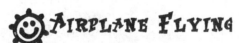

☺ AIRPLANE FLYING

Place Paper Airplanes (Props to Make) in the
center and encourage children to try flying them.

Skills To Build
• Small motor development
• Spatial awareness

185

☀ Literature List

☺ Picture Books

• *Airplanes*
by Byron Barton;
Harper LB 1986. (PS)
Simple words and brightly colored
artwork introduce airplanes.

• *Flying*
by Donald Crews;
Greenwillow LB 1986. (PS)
Brief text and colorful art highlight a
study in movement as a plane takes
off, flies over landscapes, and lands.

• *Planes*
by Anne Rockwell;
Dutton 1985. (PS)
A simple introduction to airplanes
for the very young.

• *Planes*
by Angela Royston;
Macmillan 1992. (PS)
The concept of airplanes is
introduced for preschoolers in this
sturdy book with many photos.

• *Bored, Nothing to Do!*
by Peter Spier;
Doubleday 1978. (K-3)
Two bored boys put together an
airplane and fly it.

• *Airport*
by Bryon Barton
Harper LB 1992. (PS-1)
Common sights at an airport,
reproduced in drawings and text.

☺ Books to Read Aloud

• *Flying*
by Gail Gibbons;
Holiday LB 1986. (PS-1)
The history of flight from the first
balloon launch depicted in bright
colors.

• *Tim and Jim Take Off*
by Harriet Ziefert;
Viking 1993. (1-3)
Two boys take their first airplane
ride together.

• *Amelia's Fantastic Flight*
by Rose Bursik;
Henry Holt 1992. (PS-3)
Amelia flies from country to country
in the plane she has built, returning
home in time for dinner.

Plane Song
by Diane Siebert;
Harper LB 1993. (PS-2)
A variety of airplanes are introduced
in rhyming verse and oil paintings.

• *Redbird*
by Patrick Fort;
Orchard 1988. (PS-3)
Redbird, an airplane, flies through a
thunderstorm but can't land until
the weather clears.

• *Salty Takes Off*
by Gloria Rand;
Henry Holt 1991. (K-3)
Salty Dog accompanies an aviator
when he delivers air mail to isolated
logging camps in Alaska.

Theme Centers for Dramatic Play

RESOURCES & MORE

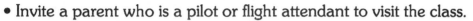

RESOURCES & RELATED ACTIVITIES

- Invite a parent who is a pilot or flight attendant to visit the class.

- Invite a travel agent to visit the class.

- Take a short ride on the local train.

- Visit an airport to watch the planes take off.

- Invite a model plane builder to bring his models to class to share.

- Invite a parent who has travelled by train to share her experience (pictures, memorabilia) with the class.

- Visit a transportation museum.

- If you are under a landing pattern, make a frequency chart of the number of planes that fly over.

- Find out when a large freight train passes through your area. Go and watch it.

- Visit a local train depot.

- Make a chart showing how often children in your class and/or their parents fly.

- Share picture books about other forms of transportation.

- Try flying a variety of paper airplanes. Make a distance chart showing the area traveled.

187

Dear Parents:

We are preparing a Flight of Fancy Theme Center in our classroom during these dates: _____. This center will provide an opportunity for the children to participate in dramatic play and will serve as a basis for classroom discussion and learning activities. Below you will find a list of items that we need to furnish the center:

☐ Margarine lids   ☐ Travel brochures

☐ Tongue depressors   ☐ Magazines

☐ Old suitcase   ☐ Discarded airline ticket

☐ Old briefcase   ☐ Baggage tags

☐ Maps   ☐ _____

Please return the items checked above by _____.

You can support the use of this center by talking to your child about the theme, planning family excursions related to the theme, or by sharing books that will provide your child with more information. A suggested literature list is available upon request.

Parent Name _____

Phone Number _____ ☐ I would love to help!

© Edupress   *Theme Centers for Dramatic Play*

POST OFFICE

© Edupress   Theme Centers for Dramatic Play

CENTER SET-UP

FLOORPLAN

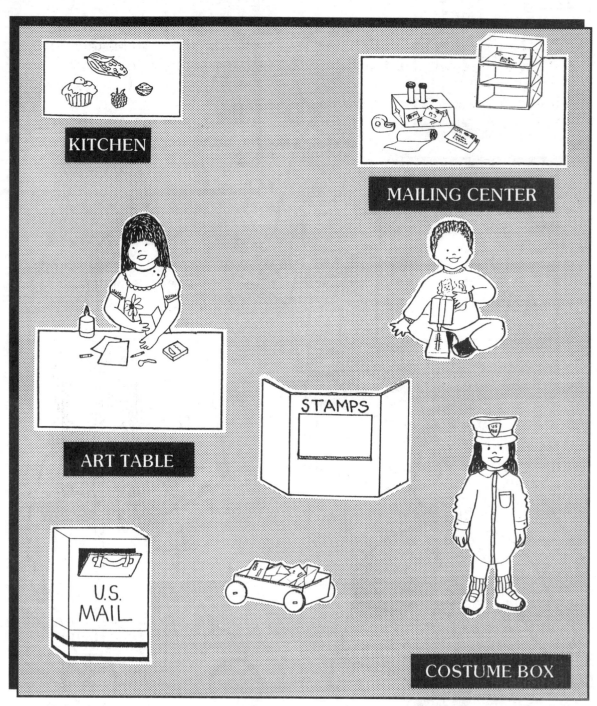

KITCHEN

MAILING CENTER

ART TABLE

STAMPS

U.S. MAIL

COSTUME BOX

190

Center Set-Up

Furnishings And Accessories

Miscellaneous
- Mail cart (Props to Make)
- Mail box (Bare-Budget Furnishings)
- Postage stamp window (Bare-Budget Furnishings)
- Post office boxes (Props to Make)
- Baby buggy, doll clothes, & blankets

Post Office Kitchen
- Dishes
- Play food
- Silverware
- Lunch boxes

Costume Box
- Jackets
- Hats
- Sweaters
- Dresses
- Shorts
- Caps

Mailing Center
- Stickers (resembling stamps)
- Mail Bag (Props to Make)
- Pens and pencils in cups
- Envelopes
- Paper
- Balance or postal scale
- Telephone books
- Zip code book
- Catalogs
- Advertising flyers

Art Table
- Box of cancelled postage stamps (Activity—Postage Stamp Collage)
- Rubber stamps
- Stamp pads

191

Center Set-Up

Bare-Budget Furnishings

Postage Stamp Window

Materials
- Large cardboard box
- Scissors
- Exacto knife

Directions
1. Cut away one side, the top and bottom of the cardboard box.
3. Cut away rectangle from top half of center panel to create postal stamp window.

Mail Box

Materials
- Large cardboard box
- Small cardboard box
- Masking tape
- Scissors

Directions
1. Cut off bottom of large box.
2. Seal all open sides of box with masking tape.
3. Cut one side as shown in diagram.
4. Use a small piece of cardboard taped on box as shown for handle.
5. Place small box inside large box to catch mail.

192

Center Enhancements

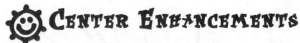

Cost of Package Mailing Chart

Use tagboard to create a chart showing the weight and size of a package with individual mailing cost. Use a U.S. map and color code map and chart. Supply a scale and measuring tape.

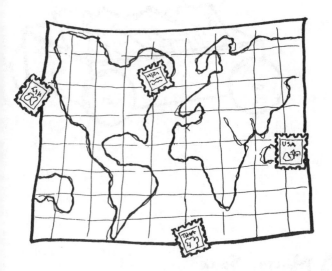

World Map

Put map up on the wall. Ask parent stamp-collectors to supply cancelled foreign stamps. Put stamp on appropriate country.

Envelope

Use butcher paper to create a large envelope front and mount it on the wall. Use as a sign for the center name.

Props to Make

☀ Mail Cart

Materials
- Cardboard box, 2 feet x 2 feet (61 cm x 61 cm)
- 2 ½-inch (6 cm) dowels, 2½ feet (.76 m) long
- 4 brass brads or thumb tacks

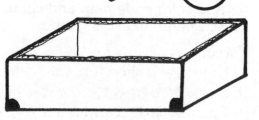

Directions
1. Cut upper flaps off cardboard box (save).
2. Outline dowel end on all four corners of box.
3. Cut around outlines and insert dowels through openings.
4. Cut four wheels from saved flaps.
5. Attach wheels on dowel ends using brads or thumb tacks.

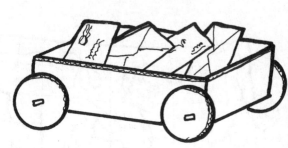

☀ Mail Bag

Materials
- Large sheet of construction paper
- 2 pieces of yarn, 36 inches (1 m) long
- Hole punch
- Stapler
- Markers

Directions
1. Fold construction paper in half.
2. Punch holes in the four corners.
3. Tie yarn in holes as shown.
4. Staple sides together and decorate with markers.

194

Theme Centers for Dramatic Play

PROPS TO MAKE

POST OFFICE BOXES

Materials
- Shoe boxes
- Stickers
- Stapler
- Contact paper
- Markers

Directions
1. Cover each shoe box with contact paper.
2. Stack shoe boxes and staple together.
3. Decorate exterior with markers and stickers.

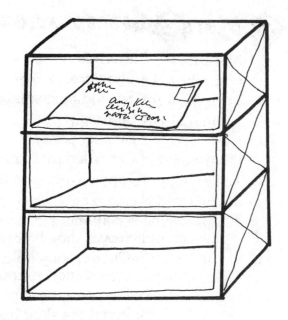

CANCELLATION STAMP

Materials
- 4-inch (10 cm) x 1½-inch (3.8 cm) dowel
- Pink eraser
- Paring knife
- Tacky glue
- Sandpaper

Directions
1. Sand dowel smooth.
2. Using paring knife, carve a design in the eraser (see suggested designs).
3. Glue eraser onto end of dowel.

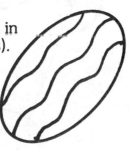

195

PROPS TO MAKE

☼ CANCELLATION STAMP HOLDER

Materials
- Shoe box
- Second box, smaller than shoe box
- Scissors
- Butcher paper
- Cancelled mail items
- Tape

Directions
1. Cover shoe box with butcher paper.
2. Cut as many holes in bottom of shoe box as you have cancellation stamps.
3. Decorate the shoe box with pieces of cancelled mail.
4. Invert the shoe box over the smaller box. The smaller box will support the cancellation stamps.

196

Theme Centers for Dramatic Play

Teaching Tips

☀ Center Tips

Introducing the Center
During circle time talk about getting mail at home. Ask about when they get mail (birthday, holidays, get-well). Discuss how mail gets to you. Ask questions regarding post office workers.

Safety Tips
• Remind the children that they cannot lean on the postage stamp window—it will fall over.

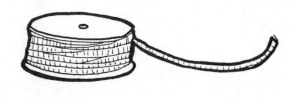

☀ Center Variations

Wrap and Mail Store
• Put out gift wrap and ribbons with boxes to mail packages.
• Add foam "peanuts" for packing.

Stationery Store
• Provide boxes of stationery and greeting cards.
• Put out rubber stamps and stamp pads.
• Add a cash register.

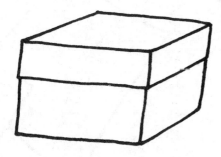

Developmental Activities

Letter Writing

Use materials on the art table to make pieces of mail—letters, advertisements, cards, etc. Store in mail bag or deposit into mail box.

Skills To Build
- Small motor
- Sorting skills

Stationery Creations

Cut paper into a variety of sizes and place on art table. Allow children to decorate and/or write letters.

Skills To Build
- Language development
- Art exploration

198

DEVELOPMENTAL ACTIVITIES

☀ WEIGH-IN

Put out a variety of packages and letters of different sizes. Let children use the postal scale to compare weights.

Skills To Build
• Seriation
• Number concepts
• Small motor

☀ POSTAGE STAMP COLLAGE

Set out a large piece of tagboard and some glue sticks. Put a box of cancelled stamps on the table. Invite the children to make a collage on the tagboard using the glue sticks and stamps.

Skills To Build
• Small motor development
• Visual discrimination

199

LITERATURE LIST

PICTURE BOOKS

• *How Paper is Made*
by Neil Curtis & Peter Greenland;
Lerner LB 1992. (K-3)
In easy language, the book explains
how loggers cut down trees, and the
process of making paper.

• *Mr. Griggs Work*
by Cynthia Rylant;
Orchard 1989. (PS-2)
Mr. Griggs, who works at the post
office, loves his work.

• *Paper, Paper Everywhere*
by Gail Gibbons;
Harcourt 1983. (PS-2)
A picture-book that shows how
useful and ever-present is paper.

• *Here Comes the Mail*
by Gloria Skyzynski;
Macmillan 1982. (K-3)
Shows how the postal system works
by telling how Stephanie can send a
letter to her cousin miles away.

• *The Post Office Book: Mail and
How It Moves*
by Gail Gibbons;
Harper LB 1982. (K-3)
A simple description of how the post
office works.

• *A Visit to the Post Office*
by Sandra Ziegler;
Children's LB 1989. (1-3)
Scott and his school class visit the
local post office.

BOOKS TO READ ALOUD

• *Don't Forget to Write*
by Martina Selway;
Ideals 1992. (PS-2)
On a visit to Grandad's farm, Rosie
writes letters daily to her mother.

• *Snowshoe Thompson*
by Nancy S. Levinson;
Harper LB 1991. (1-2)
This true story tells about a postman
and how he delivers a letter in spite
of mountains of snow.

• *No Mail for Mitchell*
by Catherine Siracusa;
Random 1990. (K-1)
The postman, a dog named
Mitchell, never gets any letters for
himself.

• *Stamps*
by Karen Jacobsen;
Childrens LB 1983. (K-3)
The history and use of stamps in a
simple, well-organized account.

• *Flat Stanley*
by Jeff Brown;
Harper LB 1964. (1-3)
A falling bulletin board flattens
Stanley so he's only one-half-inch
thick.

• *Special Delivery*
by Betty Brandt;
Carolrhoda LB 1988. (1-3)
The U.S. Post Office system and
how it developed.

RESOURCES & MORE

RESOURCES & RELATED ACTIVITIES

- Locate postage stamp posters.

- Take a field trip to the post office.

- Write a letter, put a stamp on it and walk to the nearest mailbox to mail it.

- Invite a letter carrier (possibly a parent) to come and visit the classroom.

- Arrange a field trip to a "wrap and mail" store.

- Invite a stamp collector to come and share his or her collection with the class.

- Find a variety of maps and share them with the class.

- Plan a field trip to a stationery store.

- Design a postage stamp.

- Have each child bring the address of a grandparent or other family member, and locate the city or state on the map. (See page 11—Map Tracking.)

- Make a collection of "junk mail," using it to spark a discussion of conservation and recycling.

- Make a collection of the different kinds of things that come in the mail.

201

Dear Parents:

We are preparing a Post Office Theme Center in our classroom during these dates: _____. This center will provide an opportunity for the children to participate in dramatic play and will serve as a basis for classroom discussion and learning activities. Below you will find a list of items that we need to furnish the center:

☐ Shoe boxes   ☐ Greeting cards

☐ Envelopes   ☐ Balance-postal scale

☐ Stationery   ☐ Rubber stamps and stamp pads

☐ Maps   ☐ Cancelled postage stamps

☐ Stickers   ☐ _____

Please return the items checked above by _____.

You can support the use of this center by talking to your child about the theme, planning family excursions related to the theme, or by sharing books that will provide your child with more information. A suggested literature list is available upon request.

Parent Name _____

Phone Number _____ ☐ I would love to help!

202

Kid Care Clinic

203

Theme Centers for Dramatic Play

Center Set-Up

Floorplan

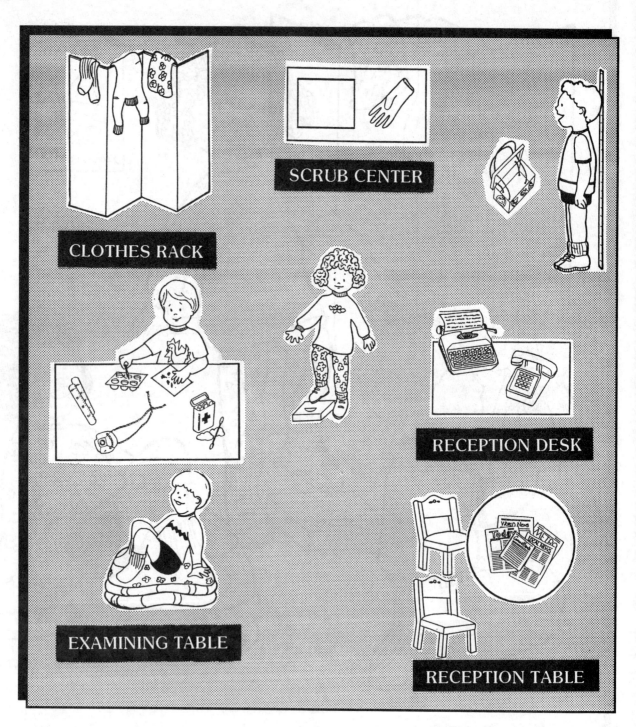

CLOTHES RACK

SCRUB CENTER

RECEPTION DESK

EXAMINING TABLE

RECEPTION TABLE

204

Theme Centers for Dramatic Play

CENTER SET-UP

☀ FURNISHINGS AND ACCESSORIES

Scrub Center
- Clear jars holding:
  - ace bandage
  - gauze roll
  - band-aids
  - tongue depressor
  - cotton balls
- Soap
- Paper cups
- Facial tissues
- Paper towels
- Paper patient gowns or aprons
- Rubber gloves

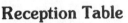

Art Table
- Eye droppers (Activity page—Eye Dropper Art)
- Poster board
- Assortment swabs, cotton balls, gauze and tongue depressors (Activity page—First Aid Collage)

Changing Room
- Variety of shoes
- Dresses
- White or blue dress shirt
- White aprons
- Hats
- Wallets with play money
- Nurse's Hat (Props to Make)

Reception Table
- Magazines

Reception Desk
- Telephone
- Clipboard
- Can of pencils
- Play typewriter

Examining Area
- Examining Table (Bare Budget Furnishings)
- Stethoscope (Props to Make)
- Clipboard
- Can of pencils
- Thermometer (Props to Make)

Clothes Rack (Bare Budget Furnishings)

Scale
- Provide different types of scales

205

CENTER SET-UP

☼ Bare-Budget Furnishings

Clothes Rack

If your classroom is not equipped with a standing clothes rack, try one of the following ideas:

- Open the seam on one side of a large cardboard box, set on end in "w" shape and drape clothes over it.
- String a clothesline against a wall and hang clothes on it.
- Use the classroom drying rack to drape clothes over.

Examining Mat

- Napping mats or
- Bedding or towels, folded and stacked to the desired shape and height

CENTER SET-UP

☺ CENTER ENHANCEMENTS

Height Chart

Create a height chart by taping a large piece of white butcher paper to one wall, making sure the lower edge of the paper is against the floor. Mark measurement lines at 1-inch (2.54 cm) increments.

Eye Chart

Create an eye examination chart by gluing small pictures in a pyramid shape onto a piece of white tagboard. Place on one wall of the examination area.

First Aid Posters

Display posters that show examples of good health practices, i.e., healthy eating or handwashing.

PROPS TO MAKE

 ## THERMOMETER

Materials
- Tongue depressor
- Markers
- Crayons

Directions
1. Use markers and crayons to mark mercury line and degree numbers on tongue depressor.
2. Place in examining area, reminding children that the thermometers are to look at, not to put in their mouths.

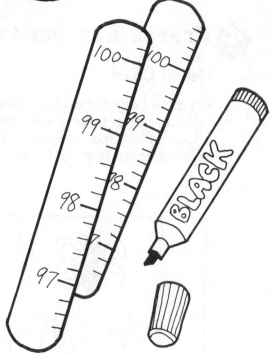

STETHOSCOPE

Materials
- Foam egg carton
- Yarn (black is best)
- Hole punch
- Masking tape

Directions
1. Cut an egg section out of carton. Punch one hole on either side.
2. Thread a 1-yard (1 m) length of yarn through the two holes.
3. Wrap masking tape around each end of the yarn. Tie ends of yarn loosely together.

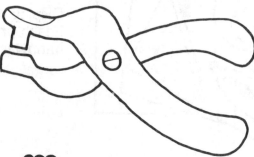

204

PROPS TO MAKE

NURSE'S HAT

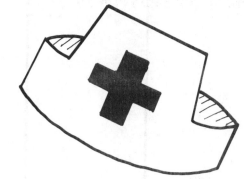

Materials
- Hat pattern (following page)
- White construction paper
- Markers
- Scissors
- Tape

Directions
1. Reproduce pattern on white construction paper.
2. Cut out.
3. Fit pieces together by matching slits in band to slits on hat piece. Secure with tape.
4. Decorate with markers.

DOCTOR'S BAG

Materials
- Shoe box
- Magazines
- Glue
- Scissors
- 2 1-yard (1 m) lengths of yarn
- Tempera paint & brush

Directions
1. Paint box and allow to dry.
2. Cut health-related pictures from magazines and glue to box.
3. Punch holes in box and lid as shown.
4. Thread 1 piece of yarn through each set of holes, as shown, and tie the ends to secure.

Theme Centers for Dramatic Play

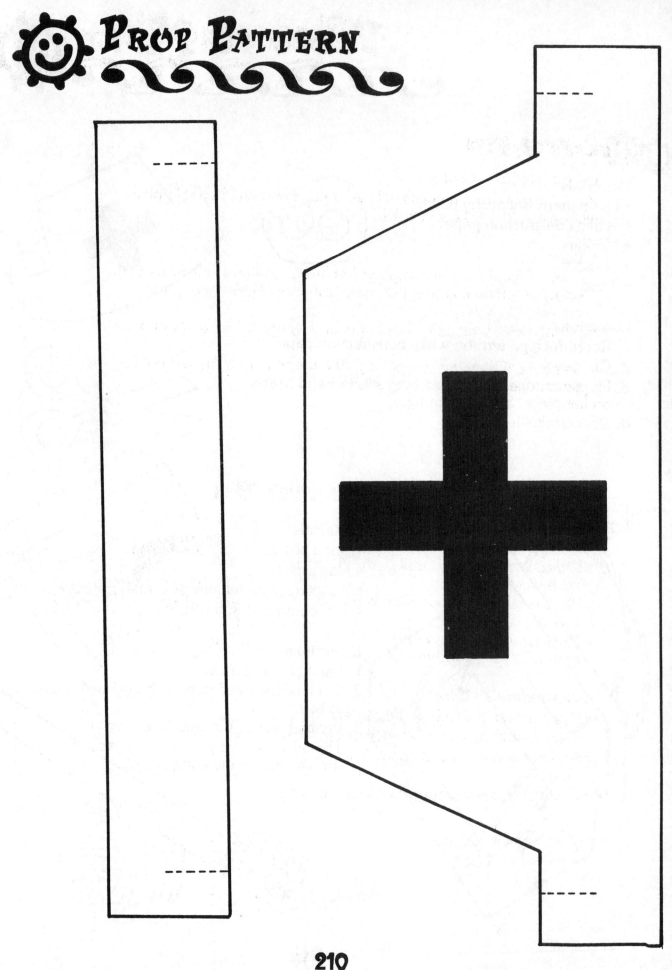

210

CENTER TIPS

Introducing the Center
Read a story about a health-related topic. Have children role-play what it would be like to be sick.

Safety Tips
• Do not include any prescription bottles or "pretend" medicine in the set-up. Remind children that only responsible grown-ups give medicine to kids.
• During circle time, talk about how and where to use gauze and ace bandages.
• Remind children that props, e.g., the thermometer, should not be put in their mouth.

CENTER VARIATIONS

Dentist's Office
• Provide a toothbrush and dental floss for each child.
• Place small, hand-held mirrors in the center.
• Place posters in the center demonstrating good dental care.

Veterinarian's Office
• Place stuffed animals in the center.
• Provide empty, clean pet food containers.
• Add pet accessories: carriers, leashes, collars.
• Move any classroom pets into the center.

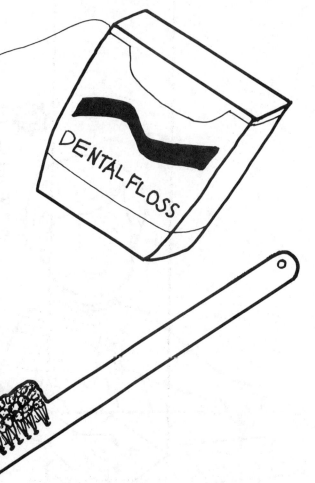

211

Developmental Activities

First Aid Collage

Provide glue and construction paper on the art table. Encourage children to make a collage of first aid items such as adhesive bandages, gauze, tissue and paper towels.

Skills To Build
- Small motor development
- Art expression
- Vocabulary development

Eye Dropper Art

Use eye droppers, pre-mixed watercolors in a muffin tin, and construction paper to make a picture.

Skills To Build
- Small motor development
- Free expression in a different art media

212

Theme Centers for Dramatic Play

Developmental Activities

☼ Weigh In

Provide one or more types of scales for children to get on and off.

Skills To Build
- Number recognition
- Value comparisons (who is taller, who weighs more)
- Balance/ motor development

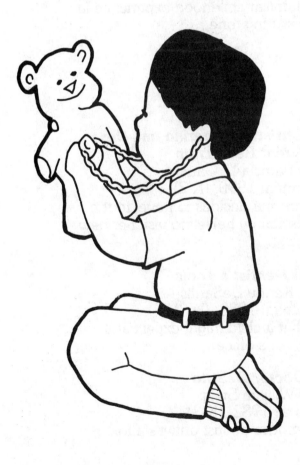

☼ Listen to a Heartbeat

Use the stethoscope (Props to Make) to pretend to listen to a heartbeat.

Skills To Build
- Body awareness
- Listening
- Counting

☼ LITERATURE LIST

☼ PICTURE BOOKS

• **When I See My Doctor**
by Susan Kuklin;
Macmillan 1988. (PS-1)
Color photos explain a routine visit
to the doctor.

• **The Picture World of
Ambulances**
by Norman Barrett;
Watts LB 1991. (K-4)
A simple introduction to
ambulances and how they are used.

• **When I See My Dentist**
by Susan Kuklin;
Macmillan 1988. (PS-1)
A realistic view of a visit to the
dentist with color photos.

• **Going to the Dentist**
by Fred Rogers;
Putnam 1989. (PS-1)
Showing that a trip to the dentist
isn't so frightening.

• **One Bear in the Hospital**
by Caroline Bucknall;
Dial 1991. (PS-K)
A young bear goes to the hospital
after an accident and has a difficult
time adjusting.

• **Going to the Doctor**
by Fred Rogers;
Putnam 1986. (PS)
A familiar childhood experience in a
reassuring tone.

☼ BOOKS TO READ ALOUD

• **My Dentist**
by Harlow Rockwell;
Greenwillow LB 1975. (1-2)
A matter-of-fact, informative book
about dentists and the instruments
they use.

• **The Emergency Room**
by Anne & Harlow Rockwell;
Macmillan 1985. (PS-1)
A simple, nonfrightening trip to the
emergency room for a boy who has
sprained his ankle.

• **A Hospital Story**
by Sara Bonnett Stein;
Walker 1984. (1-3)
A fine introduction to hospitals and
what a hospital stay involves.

• **Christina Katerina and the
Great Bear Train**
by Patricia L. Gauch;
Putnam 1990. (K-2)
Christina decides to travel to the
hospital by herself to visit her new
sibling.

• **A Dentist's Tools**
by Kenny DeSantis;
Putnam 1988. (K-3)
What a child might expect at a
dentist's office.

• **Doctor DeSoto**
by William Steig;
Farrar 1982. (K-3)
A mouse dentist outwits a fox.

214

RESOURCES & RELATED ACTIVITIES

- Take a field trip to a doctor's office.

- Invite local paramedics/doctor/ nurse/EMT to visit the classroom. (Try a parent.)

- Take a field trip to a pharmacy or drug store.

- Weigh and measure the height of each child. Make a chart that can be updated several times during the school year.

- Assemble a class first aid kit.

- Find where your pulse is on your wrist, then practice on the classroom animals.

- Ask the local doctors' offices and medical centers for health posters.

- Take a field trip to an optometrist's office.

- Reproduce patterns for children to make their own nurse's hats (Props to Make).

- Learn songs about health and safety.

- Use small spoons to scoop or count ingredients into zip-top bags to make a healthy snack. Ingredients can include: cereal, raisins, pretzels, peanuts, coconut.

- Role-play giving first aid to a hurt child.

- Have a "health day" at school—measure and weigh each child, bring a real stethoscope to try out.

- Provide supplies at the examining table and invite children to make their own thermometers.

Dear Parents:

  We are preparing a Kid Care Clinic Theme Center in our classroom during these dates: _____. This center will provide an opportunity for the children to participate in dramatic play and will serve as a basis for classroom discussion and learning activities. Below you will find a list of items that we need to furnish the center:

☐ Gauze rolls   ☐ 2 x 2-inch (5 x 5 cm) gauze squares

☐ Adhesive bandages   ☐ Tongue depressors

☐ Magazines   ☐ Clear glass jars

☐ Cotton balls   ☐ Ace bandages

☐ Rubber gloves   ☐ _____

  Please return the items checked above by _____.

  You can support the use of this center by talking to your child about the theme, planning family excursions related to the theme, or by sharing books that will provide your child with more information. A suggested literature list is available upon request.

Parent Name _____

Phone Number _____ ☐ I would love to help!

216

Theme Centers for Dramatic Play

Theme Centers for Dramatic Play

CENTER SET-UP

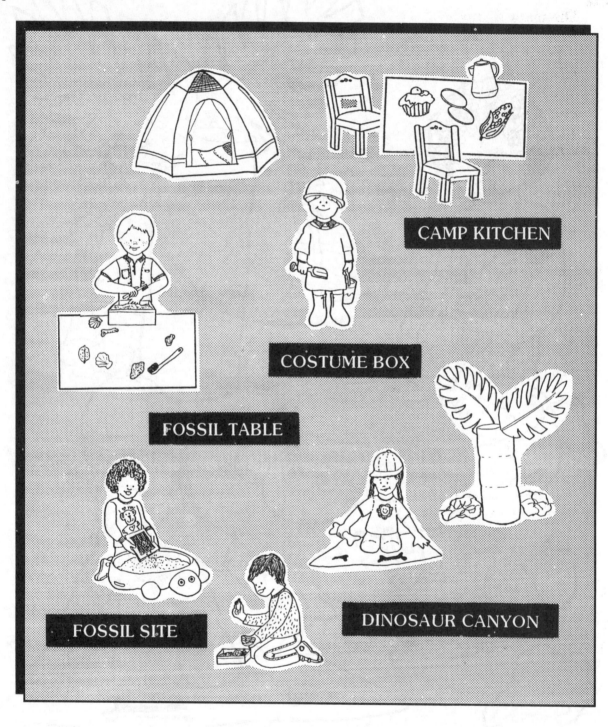

CAMP KITCHEN

COSTUME BOX

FOSSIL TABLE

DINOSAUR CANYON

FOSSIL SITE

218

☼ FURNISHINGS AND ACCESSORIES

Dinosaur Canyon
- Dinosaur Canyon Cloth (Bare-Budget Furnishings)
- Dinosaur Bones (Props to Make)

Fossil Table
- Excavation Boxes (Props to Make)
- Art materials

Camp Kitchen
- Dishes
- Coffee pot
- Canteens

Fossil Site (Bare-Budget Furnishings)
- Sand Sifters (Props to Make)
- Fossils (Props to Make)
- Small Shovels
- Buckets

Costume Box
- Pith helmets
- Baseball caps
- Hard hats (plastic bowls)
- White shirts (lab jackets)
- T-shirts

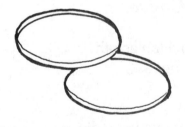

Center Set-Up

Bare-Budget Furnishings

Fossil Site
Materials
- Hard-sided swimming/wading pool
- Vinyl drop cloth
- Clean sand

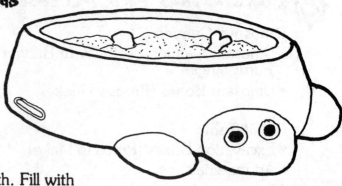

Directions
Position pool in the center of drop cloth. Fill with sand. Use as a site for "burying" fossils, Dinosaur Bones (Props to Make) and artifacts.

Dinosaur Canyon
Materials
- Square vinyl tablecloth
- Contact paper

Directions
1. Cut one or two large dinosaur shapes from contact paper.
2. Use bone patterns (page 214) to cut several bone shapes from contact paper.
3. Stick all contact paper shapes to tablecloth .

☼ CENTER ENHANCEMENTS

Desert Oasis

Use tempera paint and butcher paper to create a background scene of a sandy desert and an oasis pool.

Palm Tree

Make a column with round half-gallon ice cream containers. Use duct tape to secure. Paint brown or cover with brown paper. Cut palm fronds from green butcher paper and tape to top of column.

Sleeping Quarters

Create a diggers' camp by putting up a small dome tent with a sleeping bag inside and a camp stool outside the door.

Excavation Location

Crumple brown paper grocery bags and attach them to the wall around the painted background scene to simulate a cave or rocky digging site.

PROPS TO MAKE

☀ SAND SIFTER

Materials
- 8 x 8-inch (20 x 20 cm) square of fabric netting or screen
- 2 pieces of heavy cardboard, 8 x 8-inch (20 x 20 cm) square
- Exacto® knife
- Stapler

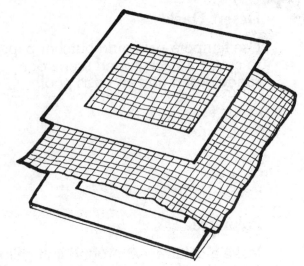

Directions
1. Use knife to cut a square opening in each cardboard piece, leaving a 1-inch (2.54 cm) "frame."
2. Place netting between the layers of cardboard and staple together.

☀ EXCAVATION BOX

Materials
- Large shoe box with lid
- Clean sand
- Toothbrush or small paintbrush
- Fossils or other small objects

Directions
1. Fill shoe box with sand.
2. "Bury" fossils and other objects in the sand. Place toothbrush or paintbrush on top of sand and put lid on box.

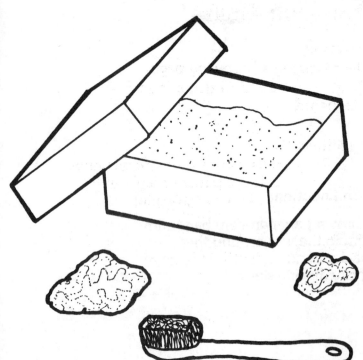

222

Theme Centers for Dramatic Play

Props to Make

☼ Fossils

Materials
- Self-hardening clay
- Small plastic dinosaurs, plastic animals, or natural items such as leaves, acorns, or shells
- Baking sheet
- Plastic knife

Directions
1. Pat clay out on baking sheet.
2. Use plastic animals or natural objects to make impressions in the dough.
3. Cut into irregular shapes with knife.
4. Allow clay to harden.

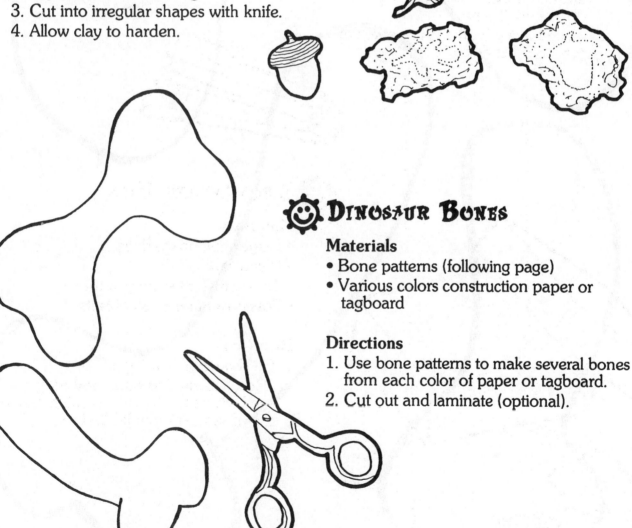

☼ Dinosaur Bones

Materials
- Bone patterns (following page)
- Various colors construction paper or tagboard

Directions
1. Use bone patterns to make several bones from each color of paper or tagboard.
2. Cut out and laminate (optional).

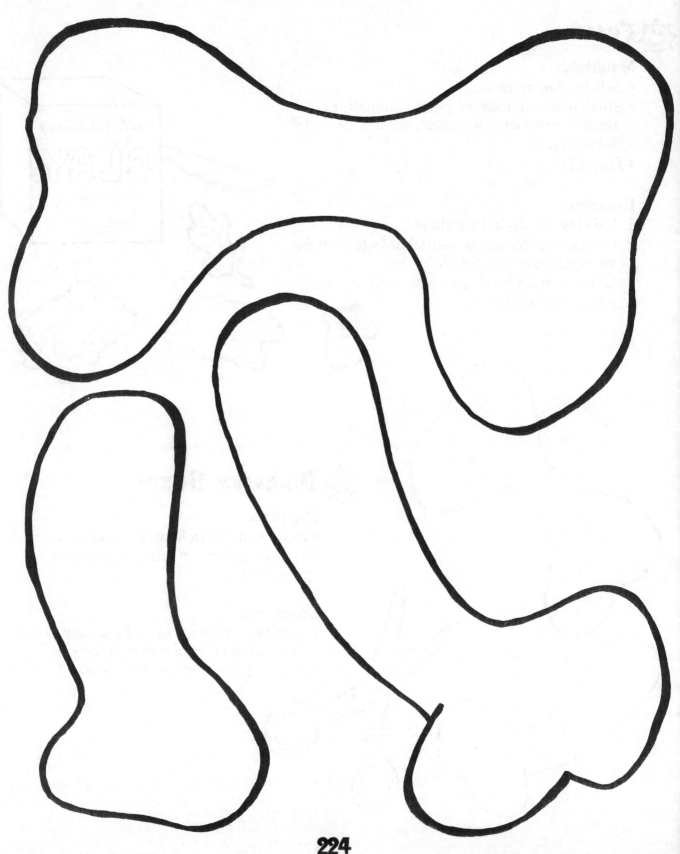

224

Theme Centers for Dramatic Play

Center Tips

Introducing the Center
During circle time, share an interesting fossil sample or geode. Open an excavation box and let one of the children help you explore it. Ask children about any trips they may have taken to museums to see dinosaur bones.

Safety Tips
- Remind children that sand must remain in the sand area and the Excavation Boxes
- Demonstrate the proper and safe use of any tools in the center.
- Remind children that sand must not be thrown.

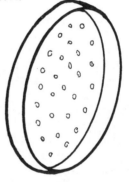

Center Variations

Natural History Museum
Gather other exhibits such as shell or insect collections. Arrange on center tables with books about these subjects.

At the Beach
Add sand buckets, shovels, sand toys, and sifters to transform the fossil site into a beach. Include beach towels and an umbrella plus magnifying glasses for examining seashells and rocks.

225

 Developmental Activities

☺ Dinosaur Dig

Explore the contents of Excavation Boxes (Props to Make) to find items that you might find while digging for dinosaurs!

Skills To Build
• Object identification

☺ Fossil Match

Store Fossils (Props to Make) and the objects used to make them in a container together. Encourage children to match the clay fossils with the object that made the imprint.

Skills To Build
• Visual discrimination
• Comparing and contrasting
• Matching

226

Theme Centers for Dramatic Play

DEVELOPMENTAL ACTIVITIES

BONE PILE

Sort and stack dinosaur bones. Match by color or size. Use bones to create a dinosaur shape or match to the shapes on the tablecloth in Dinosaur Canyon (Bare-Budget Furnishings).

Skills To Build
- Sorting
- Matching
- Size discrimination
- Color identification

SIFTING SAND

Use Sand Sifters (Props to Make) to discover objects in the sandbox.

Skills To Build
- Small motor skills
- Tactile awareness
- Size comparison

© Edupress *Theme Centers for Dramatic Play*

LITERATURE LIST

PICTURE BOOKS

• **Archaeology**
by Dennis B. Fradin;
Childrens LB 1983. (1-4)
A very broad topic competently
introduced for primary grades.

• **Dinosaurs and Their Relatives
  in Action**
by Gay O. Tanner;
Macmillan 1991. (K-3)
A pop-up book that gives solid
information about prehistoric
animals.

• **Dinosaur Dig**
by Kathryn Lasky;
Morrow LB 1990. (1-6)
Describes a family's experiences on
a paleontological dig.

• **Dinosaurs, Dragonflies and
  Diamonds: All About Natural
  History Museums**
by Gail Gibbons;
Macmillan 1988 (PS-2)
Introducing exhibits and collections
in a natural history museum.

• **Dinosaur Bones**
by Aliki;
Harper LB 1988. (PS-3)
Discovery of fossils and the theories
that emerged about their meaning.

• **Dinosaur Dreams**
by Allan Ahlberg;
Greenwillow LB 1991. (PS-2)
Three skeletons dream about
battling prehistoric animals.

BOOKS TO READ ALOUD

• **Will's Mammoth**
by Rafe Martin;
Putnam 1989. (K-2)
Will travels back in time to when
mammoths and saber-toothed tigers
roamed the earth.

• **Mik's Mammoth**
by Roy Gerrard;
Farrar 1990. (K-3)
Mik the caveman is called a coward,
but he proves himself when he is
separated from the others.

• **Ugh**
by Richard Yorinks;
Farrar 1990. (PS-3)
During prehistoric times, a young
boy named Ugh invents the first
bicycle.

• **Stanley**
by Syd Hoff;
Harper LB 1992. (1-3)
A caveman finds a new home in this
inventive tale.

• **Dinosaur for a Day**
by Jim Murphy;
Scholastic 1992. (K-3)
A mother dinosaur and her eight
children search for food on a lush
island.

• **Dinosaur Valley**
by Mitsuhiro Kurokawa;
Chronicle LB 1992. (K-4)
Readers go on a trip to Dinosaur
Valley millions of years ago.

Theme Centers for Dramatic Play

RESOURCES & RELATED ACTIVITIES

- Visit a natural history museum.

- Look for any local restoration or archaeological digging sites and arrange for a tour.

- Go on a rock hunt in the school yard. Compare the characteristics of the rocks found.

- Let children make their own "Geologic Sculptures" (page 221). Provide containers of different types of soil and show them how to make layers in small glass jars.

- Make fossils by imprinting small objects in clay or salt dough.

- Conduct a sensory activity by feeling different types of soil placed in plastic tubs:
  - sand
  - mud
  - potting soil
  - planter dirt

- Use a magnifying glass to examine bones obtained from the butcher shop.

- Learn several dinosaur names.

- Head outside with shovels and develop motor skills by digging in the school sandbox and planter areas.

229

Dear Parents:

We are preparing a Dinosaur Dig Theme Center in our classroom during these dates: _____. This center will provide an opportunity for the children to participate in dramatic play and will serve as a basis for classroom discussion and learning activities. Below you will find a list of items that we need to furnish the center:

☐ Nylon net   ☐ Square vinyl tablecloth

☐ Toy shovels   ☐ Plastic animals

☐ Toy buckets   ☐ Plastic dinosaurs

☐ Sand   ☐ Small paint brush

☐ Shoe boxes   ☐ _____

Please return the items checked above by _____.

You can support the use of this center by talking to your child about the theme, planning family excursions related to the theme, or by sharing books that will provide your child with more information. A suggested literature list is available upon request.

Parent Name _____

Phone Number _____ ☐ I would love to help!

Bloomers Garden Center

CENTER SET-UP

DIRT TABLE

WATER TABLE

GREEN HOUSE

ART SHELF

COSTUME BOX

232

Theme Centers for Dramatic Play

CENTER SET-UP

☀ FURNISHINGS AND ACCESSORIES

Art Shelf
- Plant stakes (tongue depressors)
- Rubber stamps
- Stamp pads
- Cut-up fabric
- Tacky glue

Water Table
- Strawberry baskets
- Watering cans
- Measuring scoops
- Spray bottles

Dirt Table
- (Change dirt to seeds, sand, decorative gravel)
- Measuring cups
- Various jars, boxes

Costume Box
- Sun Hats (Props to Make)
- Aprons
- Garden gloves
- Visors
- Galoshes

Green House (Bare-Budget Furnishings)
- Seed packets
- Plastic flower pots w/soil
- Watering can
- Potting Table (Bare-Budget Furnishings)

Kitchen Unit
- Plastic flower pots
- Multi-section pots
- Trowels
- Cultivators
- Baskets

Miscellaneous
- Seed catalogs
- Almanacs
- Gardening books

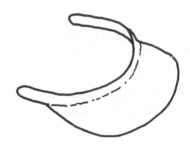

233

CENTER SET-UP

BARE-BUDGET FURNISHINGS

Green House
Materials
- 10 pieces PVC pipe, each 5 feet (1.52 m) long
- PVC connectors, four 90°-elbows & four T-elbows
- 8 large leaf bags
- Duct tape
- Scissors

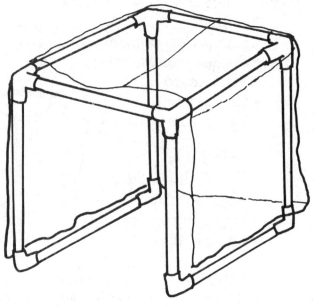

Directions
1. Assemble PVC frame as shown.
2. Cut leaf bags so that they lie flat.
3. Tape six leaf bags over upper PVC pieces and allow them to drape down.
4. Tape two leaf bags across the top to form the roof.

Potting Table
Materials
- Long, 2-foot (61 cm) high cardboard box
- 2 large leaf bags
- Duct tape
- Scissors

Directions
1. Use duct tape to tape cardboard box shut.
2. Cut leaf bags so that they lie flat.
3. Cover cardboard box with leaf bags using duct tape.

234

Theme Centers for Dramatic Play

CENTER SET-UP

CENTER ENHANCEMENTS

Flower Background Mural

Paint the bottom half of an 8-foot (2.44 m) section of butcher paper with green paint. Attach it to the wall or fence.

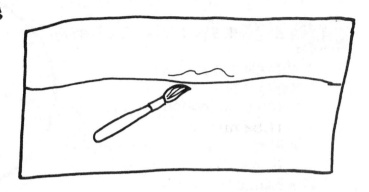

Plant Sale Flyers

Use construction paper folded in half to create plant sale flyers. Either cut pictures of flowers and plants from magazines, or draw flowers and plants on the construction paper.

Mini-Terrariums

Cut off the top half of a liter soda bottle and discard. Fill the bottom half with potting soil. (May be covered with zip-lock bags.) Plant small house plants in the soil.

Flower Arranging Basket

Cut pieces of Styrofoam™ to fit into strawberry baskets. Arrange some artificial flowers in one or two of them.

PROPS TO MAKE

☀ SUN HATS

Materials
- Tagboard
- 1 yard (1 m) ribbon
- Scissors
- Stapler

Directions
1. Cut a circle out of the tagboard.
2. Cut out a 2-inch (5 cm) wedge from one side.
3. Pull two sides together and staple closed.
4. Poke holes in tagboard as indicated at X.
5. Thread ribbon through holes so that it will tie below the chin.

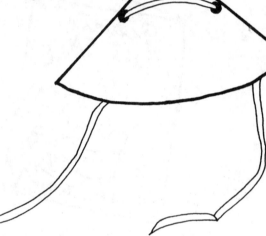

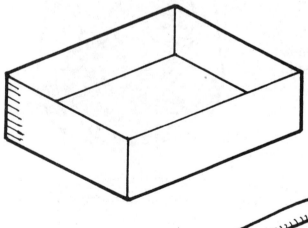

☀ PLANT FLAT

Materials
- Cardboard flat from case of soda
- Tempera paint
- Paint roller

Directions
If it is necessary to cover label information, paint the cardboard box using a roller.

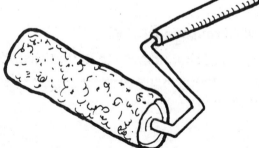

236

Props to Make

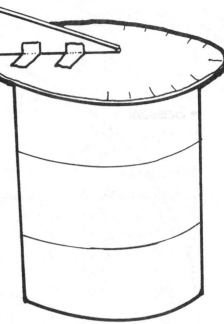

☼ Sun Dial

Materials
- Pattern (following page)
- Duct Tape
- Scissors
- Coffee can
- Cardboard
- Markers

Directions
1. Use pattern to cut pieces from cardboard.
2. Attach circle to coffee can with duct tape.
3. Tape cardboard triangle upright on straight line marked on sundial face.

☼ Rain Gauge

Materials
- Small bottled water container
- Small saw or serrated knife
- Permanent markers

Directions
1. Cut away top 2 inches (5 cm) of water bottle.
2. Use permanent marker to mark water level. Start at bottom and mark each 1/4 inch (.63 cm).

☼ Pots to Plant

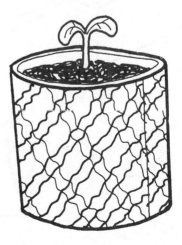

Materials
- Frozen juice can
- Hammer
- Scissors
- Contact paper
- Ice pick
- Scissors

Directions
1. Cut off top half of juice can.
2. Use ice pick and hammer to put holes in the bottom of the can.
3. Cover can with contact paper.

Prop Pattern

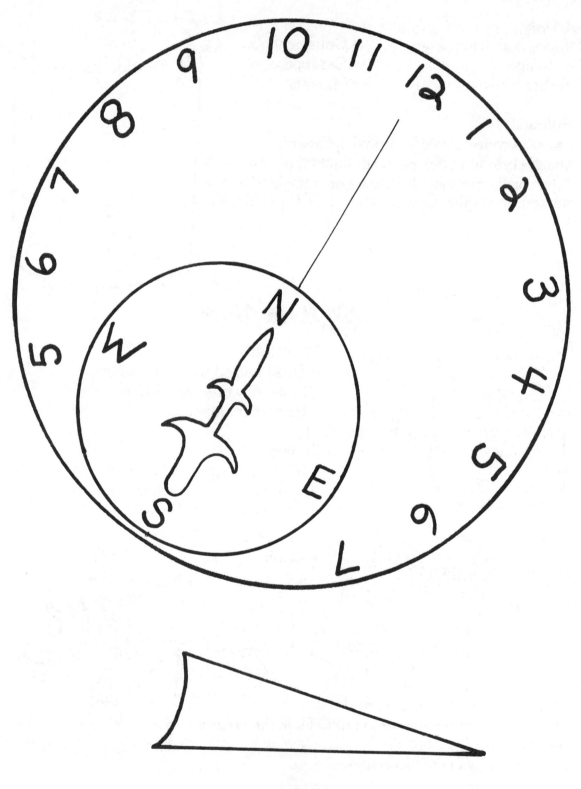

238

Theme Centers for Dramatic Play

TEACHING TIPS

☼ CENTER TIPS

Introducing the Center
One week before the unit, plant some bean seeds in a clear plastic container. On the day you wish to begin, read *The Tiny Seed* by Eric Carle. Show your own seeds after you've read the book.

Safety Tips
• Use only unbreakable plastic pots.
• Walls of Green House will collapse if they are pulled on.
• The water stays in the water table—NO SPLASHING.
• The dirt stays in the dirt table—NO THROWING.

☼ CENTER VARIATIONS

Florist Shop
Add a cash register and play money to create a Florist's Shop. Include silk flowers, tissue and wrapping paper, gift cards, and ribbon.

239

DEVELOPMENTAL ACTIVITIES

☼ PLANT SEEDS

Set out seeds in margarine tubs with the packets attached. Fill juice-can pots half-full of potting soil. Plant seed and fill pot to the top with soil.

Skills To Build
- Observing seasonal changes
- Planning and completing what one has planned

☼ MEASURE AND MOISTEN

Put potting soil in the dirt table. Add measuring tools and containers. Have water available.

Skills To Build
- Comparing amounts of one material
- Comparing attributes of two materials

240

DEVELOPMENTAL ACTIVITIES

☼ WATER WORKS

Fill the water table. Add food color. Put in a variety of tools: basters, spray bottles, sponges, margarine containers with holes in the bottom.

Skills To Build
- Tactile experience
- Small motor skills
- Manipulating and combining materials
- Investigating attributes

☼ PLANT PACK

Fill Plant Flats (Props to Make) with Pots (Props to Make). How many pots fit in the flat?

Skills To Build
- Counting
- Size comparison
- Spatial awareness

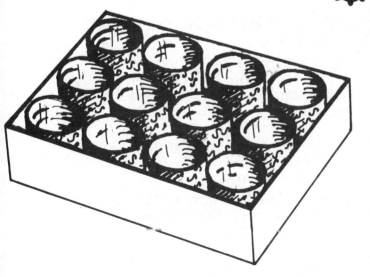

241

LITERATURE LIST

PICTURE BOOKS

• **In My Garden**
by Ermano Cristini & Luigi Puricelli;
Picture Book 1991. (PS-2)
A journey across a garden where a variety of plants, animals, and insects live.

• **In My Garden: A Child's Gardening Book**
by Helen Oeschli;
Macmillan 1985. (PS-1)
Beginners learn how to get a vegetable garden started.

• **A Very Young Gardener**
by Jill Krementz;
Dial LB 1991. (K-3)
Color photos follow a 6-year-old gardener at work.

• **From Seed to Plant**
by Gail Gibbons;
Holiday 1991. (PS-3)
How seeds grow into plants and how flowering plants produce seeds.

• **Plants**
Dorling 1992. (PS-1)
The internal parts of plants are shown in simple text and diagrams that peel back to reveal the insides.

• **Green Beans**
by Elizabeth Thomas;
Carolrhoda LB 1992. (PS-2)
Gramma, who is trying too hard to make her green beans grow, lets granddaughter Dorothea take over.

BOOKS TO READ ALOUD

• **Pumpkin Pumpkin**
by Jeanne Titherington;
Greenwillow LB 1986. (PS-1)
A simple, rhythmic picture book about the facts of plant life.

• **Garden Partners**
by Diane Palmisciano;
Macmillan LB 1989. (PS-2)
A traditional grandmother and her very modern granddaughter tend a garden together.

• **Grandpa's Garden Lunch**
by Judith Casely;
Greenwillow LB 1990. (PS-2)
Sarah helps her grandfather garden, and later Grandma makes a lunch with the fruits and vegetables from their work.

• **Festus and Mercury: Ruckus in the Garden**
by Sven Nordqvist;
Carolrhoda LB 1991. (1-3)
Festus and his cat have trouble gardening.

• **The Garden in the City**
by Gerda Muller;
Dutton 1992. (PS-3)
Caroline and Ben turn the lawn of their old house in the city into a wonderful garden.

• **Kenny's Window**
by Maurice Sendak;
Harper 1956. (K-3)
Kenny remembers a garden he has been dreaming about.

© Edupress   Theme Centers for Dramatic Play

Resources & More

Resources & Related Activities

- Visit a local nursery.

- Visit a local florist.

- Make a large chart of the sun dial. Keep a record of the progression of the sun and its shadow.

- If the weather is inclement, keep a record of the amount of rainfall over a period of days/weeks.

- Invite a parent to come and demonstrate flower arranging.

- Grow flowers or vegetables in class.

- Keep a plant growth chart of above.

- Go on a wildflower walk around school.

- Make a flower/leaf/seed/packet collage.

- Grow some vegetables and cook them (zucchini grow fast).

- Make a flower mural on the green painted butcher paper (Center Enhancements)—sponge, brush, gadget paint to make flower heads.

- Use fabric to decorate Styrofoam™ cups and then plant seeds in cups.

- Provide silk flowers to arrange in Flower Arranging Baskets (Center Enhancements).

- Find out what insects and other creatures can be found in soil and on plants. Head outside with magnifying glasses for some "close-up" investigations.

243

Dear Parents:

   We are preparing a Bloomers Garden Center Theme Center in our classroom during these dates: _____. This center will provide an opportunity for the children to participate in dramatic play and will serve as a basis for classroom discussion and learning activities. Below you will find a list of items that we need to furnish the center:

☐ Seeds   ☐ Broad-brimmed hats

☐ Seed catalogs   ☐ Watering can

☐ Small garden tools   ☐ Fabric swatches

☐ Potting soil   ☐ Plastic pots

☐ Tongue depressors   ☐ _____

Please return the items checked above by _____.

You can support the use of this center by talking to your child about the theme, planning family excursions related to the theme, or by sharing books that will provide your child with more information. A suggested literature list is available upon request.

Parent Name _____

Phone Number _____ ☐ I would love to help!

244

CAMP KID 'O VILLE

Theme Centers for Dramatic Play

CENTER SET-UP

Floorplan

TENT

CAMP KITCHEN

CAMP LOCKER

CRAFT & CREATION CORNER

FIRE RING

246

☼ Furnishings and Accessories

Miscellaneous
- Knap Sack (Props to Make)
- Clothesline
- Water bucket with spigot
- Astro Turf™
- Fishing pole
- Creel
- Compasses

Camp Kitchen
- Water jug (full)
- Dishwashing set-up, with towels, soap & water
- First Aid kit
- Dishes
- Canteen (Props to Make)

Table
- Place mats or tablecloth
- Fruit bowl
- Bird/plant/tree/flower guides
- Camp maps

Costume Box
- T-shirts
- Bandana scarves
- Duffle bags
- Sweat shirts
- Hiking shoes
- Knap sack
- Variety of hats
- Fishing vest
- Sneakers
- Flannel shirts
- Heavy socks
- Suspenders

Craft & Creation Corner
- Craft sticks
- Leaves
- Dry flowers
- Foam meat trays
- Toilet paper tubes
- Box of pebbles
- Ice cube trays

Tent (Bare-Budget Furnishings)
- Sleeping bags
- Pillows
- Pads
- Books
- Battery-powered lantern
- Flashlights

Fire Ring (Bare-Budget Furnishings)
- Water bucket
- Shovel
- Camp Mats (Props to Make)
- Bricks or large rocks
- Coffee pot
- Pot holders
- Kazoos (Props to Make)

247

CENTER SET-UP

BARE-BUDGET FURNISHINGS

Tent

Materials
- 12 sections of PVC pipe, 3-4 feet (.91-1.2 m) long
- 8 PVC elbow joints
- Covers (may be sheets, blankets, bedspread or yardage)
- Clothespins

Directions
1. Assemble the PVC pieces into the shape of a cube by joining the long pieces to one another, using the elbow joints.
2. Cover three sides and top, using chosen cover. Be sure to leave one side uncovered to serve as a door.
3. Secure coverings with clothespins.

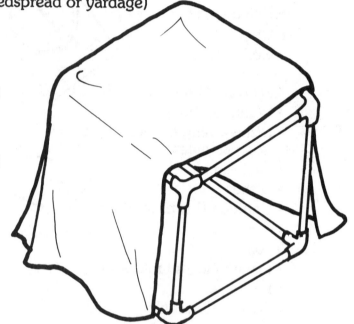

Fire Ring

Materials
- Bricks or large rocks or shoe boxes (If using boxes, prepaint brown and gray or cover with butcher paper.)
- "Presto" logs

Directions
1. Place bricks/rocks/boxes in the shape of a circle. Add logs to center to simulate a fire.
2. Decorate site with coffee pot and pot holders.

248

☼ Center Enhancements

Tree Mural

Sponge-paint an evergreen forest on butcher paper. Use several shades of green for the needles and several shades of brown for the trunks.

Single Tree

Use butcher paper cut into strips to create a tree. Twist the paper to form trunk and branches. Secure to Tree Mural. Add green paper leaves.

Hand-Washing Set-up

Tie together three 4-foot (1.2 m) long wooden poles, using cotton line. Suspend an empty gallon plastic milk container from the poles. Fill it half-full of water. Place a plastic tub below it to catch run-off.

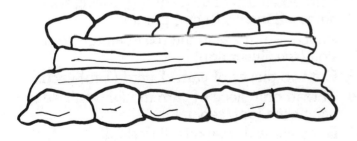

Stream

Make the bed of a stream using a blue sheet laid on the ground. Line the two banks with rocks.

Props to Make

Canteen

Materials
- Small water bottle
- Frozen juice can
- Cotton twine
- Butcher paper
- Masking tape
- Hole punch
- White glue

Directions
1. Cut top 2 inches (5 cm) off of juice can.
2. Punch two holes in the open-top end.
3. Thread twine through one hole, under bottom of can, and up through the second hole and tie ends together.
4. Secure twine on the bottom and sides of the can with tape.
5. Cover the can with butcher paper and secure with tape.
6. Put glue in the bottom inside the can and place water bottle in the can.

Knap Sack

Materials
- Brown grocery bag
- Yarn
- Markers
- Hole punch

Directions
1. Fold down top of grocery bag, rolling two times—2 inches (5 cm) per roll.
2. Punch four holes in the rolled area, two per side (see illustration).
3. Cut two pieces of yarn, 1 yard (1 m) each.
4. Thread one piece of yarn though each side, tying each loop separately.
5. Decorate with markers, if desired.

250

PROPS TO MAKE

CAMP MAT

Materials
- Pillowcase
- Newspaper
- Yarn
- Scissors
- Markers

Directions
1. Fringe both ends of the pillowcase.
2. Stuff the pillowcase with a 1 to 2-inch (2.5-5 cm) thickness of newspaper.
3. Tie fringed ends with yarn.
4. Decorate camp mat with markers.

KAZOO

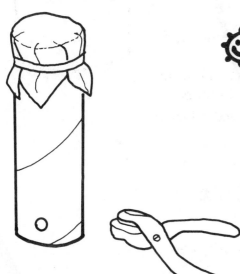

Materials
- Cardboard toilet paper center
- Waxed paper square, 3 x 3 inches (7.6 x 7.6 cm)
- Rubber band
- Hole punch

Directions
1. Punch a hole in one end of the toilet paper roll.
2. Cover the opposite end with waxed paper.
3. Gather paper and secure with rubber band.

SUN VISOR

(Prop is appropriate for child participation)
Materials
- Tagboard
- Visor pattern, following page
- Scissors
- Hole punch
- Yarn

Directions
1. Use pattern to cut visor from tagboard.
2. Punch holes where indicated. Tie a piece of yarn in each hole.
3. Decorate visor as desired.

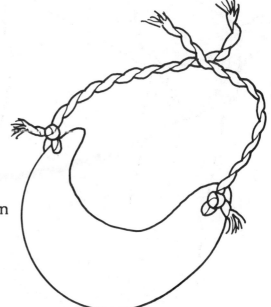

251

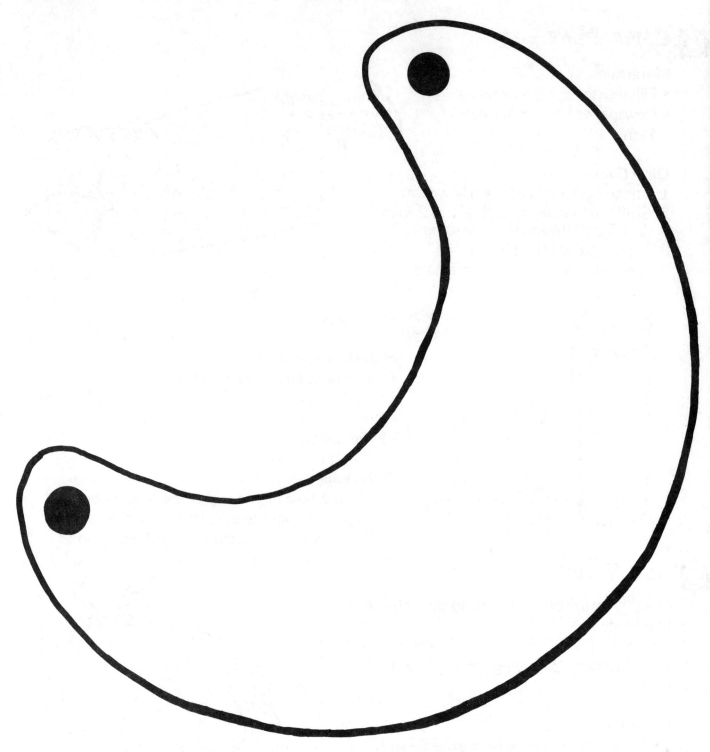

252

Theme Centers for Dramatic Play

TEACHING TIPS

☺ CENTER TIPS

Introducing the Center

During circle time, show pictures of actual camping trips accompanied by real camp gear (i.e., compass, battery, lantern rope). Ask open-ended questions about children's camping experiences and gear on hand. Be sure to dress the part yourself.

Safety Tips

- Mention that the tent is not strong enough to lean against.
- Discuss classroom fire ring safety (can be combined with real fire safety tips).
- Demonstrate the use of the handwashing station.

☺ CENTER VARIATIONS

Horse Camp/Cattle Drive

- Put a saddle and bridle on a footstool for children to "ride."
- Place cowboy boots, hats and leather gloves in the costume box.
- Provide a lariat.
- Make "brands" out of cut sponges glued to dowel ends and place in art center.
- Cover the sides of a wagon with brown butcher paper.

Jungle Safari

- Place cameras and pith helmets in center.
- Provide books with pictures of African animals.
- Decorate the center with stuffed lions, monkeys, parrots, elephants and snakes.

253

DEVELOPMENTAL ACTIVITIES

NATURE FUN

Assemble a variety of leaves, sticks, seed pods, pine cones, weeds, and flowers. Provide art materials for imaginative nature creations.

Skills To Build
• Explore actively through all the senses
• Manipulating and combining materials

CAMPFIRE MUSIC

Make a buzzing sound through the open end of a kazoo to make music. Experiment with other interesting sounds. Tapes and tape player as well as other musical instruments may also be included.

Skills To Build
• Musicality
• Sound awareness

254

DEVELOPMENTAL ACTIVITIES

PACK A KNAP SACK

Have a variety of clothing items used for camping in a bin. Provide knap sacks. Suggest children pack to go camping, letting them make their own choices. If desired, add other containers such as suitcases or duffle bags.

Skills To Build
• Manipulating objects
• Acquiring skills with equipment

PEBBLE SORTIN'

Have a variety of pebbles set out in a transparent container. Put empty ice cube trays with them. Suggest the children sort the pebbles into the trays. Let them supply the criteria for sorting.

Skills To Build
• Arranging a set of objects
• Counting
• Identifying similar properties

Edupress   *Theme Centers for Dramatic Play*

LITERATURE LIST

PICTURE BOOKS

• *Bullfrog and Gertrude Go Camping*
by Rosamond Dauer;
Dell paper 1988. (PS-1)
Bullfrog and Gertrude go camping and gain an unusual companion.

• *Camping in the Temple of the Sun*
by Deborah Gould;
Macmillan LB 1992. (PS-2)
A family's first camping trip begins poorly, but then improves.

• *Webster and Arnold Go Camping*
by P. K. Roche;
Puffin paper 1991. (PS-3)
The mouse brothers on a backyard camping trip.

• *Amos Camps Out: A Couch Adventure in the Woods*
by Susan Seligson & Howie Schneider;
Little LB 1992.(PS-3)
Amos and the couch he rarely leaves are taken on a camping trip.

• *Sleep Out*
by Carol Carrick;
Houghton 1982. (K-2)
Christopher has an unsettling experience his first night outdoors.

• *Do Not Disturb*
by Nancy Tafuri;
Greenwillow LB 1987. (PS-3)
A family camps out, unaware that they are disturbing the wildlife in the surrounding area.

BOOKS TO READ ALOUD

• *My Mom Made Me Go to Camp*
by Judy Delton;
Delacorte 1990. (1-3)
Archie, who does not want to go to camp, gradually changes his mind.

• *Starry Night*
by David Spohn;
Lothrop LB 1992. (K-2)
Nate, Matt, and Day experience their first camping trip together and marvel at all the stars in the sky.

• *You're the Scaredy Cat*
by Mercer Mayer;
Rain Bird paper 1991. (K-2)
Two young boys decide to spend the night camping out in their own back yard.

• *Petey Moroni's Camp Runamok Diary*
by Pat Cummings;
Macmillan 1992. (1-3)
At summer camp, campers discover their treats are being stolen by a raccoon.

• *Arthur's Camp-Out*
by Lillian Hoban;
Harper LB 1993. (1-2)
Arthur the chimp camps out by himself with unfortunate results.

• *Arnie Goes to Camp*
by Nancy Carlson;
Viking 1988. (1-3)
A familiar trauma of childhood is portrayed in Arnie's first "sleep-away" camp.

Resources & More

Resources & Related Activities

- Visit a local campground and tour the area.

- Ask a park ranger to come and talk to the class.

- Bring several sleeping bags to school and have children practice rolling and zipping them.

- Visit a store that sells camping supplies.

- Have an older sister/brother who is a scout come and share camping experiences.

- Go on a short nature hike near your school (city park, beach, zoo, botanical garden).

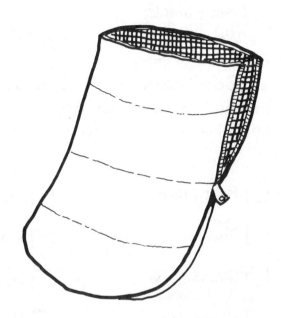

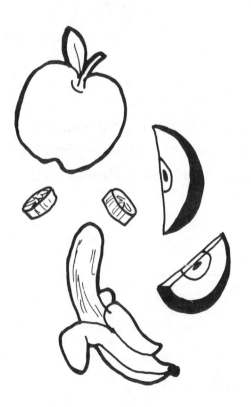

- Have a "dress for camping" day.

- Have a scavenger hunt in the school yard for "nature things." Collect in bags and share during circle time.

- Visit the beach to clean up trash (have a picnic).

- Make a map of the school yard.

- Use camp mats at the fire ring and learn some camp songs.

- Make a friendship fruit salad. Have each child bring a piece of fruit from home, cut up and combine to share at snack time.

257

Dear Parents:

We are preparing a Camp Kid 'O Ville Theme Center in our classroom during these dates: _____. This center will provide an opportunity for the children to participate in dramatic play and will serve as a basis for classroom discussion and learning activities. Below you will find a list of items that we need to furnish the center:

☐ Pillow case   ☐ Outdoor guide book

☐ Muslin   ☐ Plastic table cloth

☐ Sleeping bag   ☐ Astro Turf

☐ Binoculars   ☐ PVC pipe

☐ Compass   ☐ _____

Please return the items checked above by _____.

You can support the use of this center by talking to your child about the theme, planning family excursions related to the theme, or by sharing books that will provide your child with more information. A suggested literature list is available upon request.

Parent Name _____

Phone Number _____   ☐ I would love to help!

258

CENTER SET-UP

FLOORPLAN

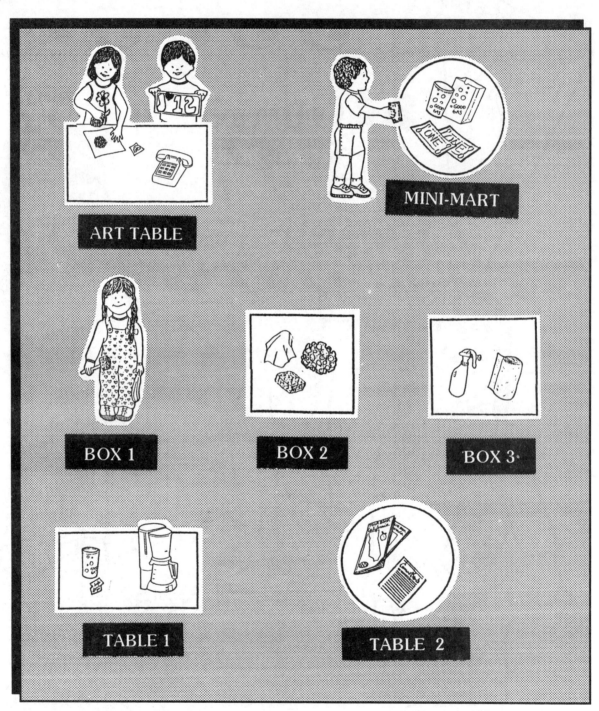

ART TABLE

MINI-MART

BOX 1

BOX 2

BOX 3

TABLE 1

TABLE 2

Center Set-Up

Furnishings and Accessories

Art Table
- Cash register
- Telephone
- Maps
- Road Sign Sponges (Props to Make)
- License Plate Frames (Props to Make)

Table 1
- Coffee cups
- Comic books
- Sugar packets
- Stir sticks
- Coffee pot

Table 2
- Magazines
- "Auto-Trader" type magazine
- Newspapers

Gas Island
- Paper towels
- Spray bottle
- Squeegee (Props to Make)

Mini-Mart
- Fast food cartons (juice boxes, soda cans, chips bags, candy wrappers)
- Play food (sandwich meat & cheese, bread, lettuce, tomato)
- Zip-lock bags
- Brown bags
- Plastic knives
- Drink cups

Box 1
- Coveralls
- Rubber shoes
- Baseball caps
- T-shirts

Box 2
- Sponges
- Rags
- Towels

Box 3
- Spray bottles
- Paper towels
- Whisk brooms

261

Center Set-Up

Bare-Budget Furnishings

Gas Pump & Nozzle
Materials
- Large cardboard box
- 3-foot (1 m) length of garden hose
- Rectangular food product box
- Toilet paper tube
- Scissors
- Knife
- Duct tape
- Markers

Directions
1. To make nozzle, cut two holes in the food box, one in the long side (#1) and one on the top (#2).
2. Insert the toilet paper tube in hole #1 and secure with tape.
3. Insert the garden hose in hole #2 and secure with tape.
4. To make pump, tape the large cardboard box closed.
5. Cut a hole in the long side to fit the diameter of the hose.
6. Insert hose and secure with tape.
7. Use markers to decorate with dials, gas station name, or logo.

Magazine Rack
Materials
- 2 cardboard boxes, 12 x 12 x 16 inches (30 x 30 x 41 cm)
- 1 shoe box
- Butcher paper
- Scissors
- Tape
- Magazines

Directions
1. Cover cardboard boxes with butcher paper.
2. Attach one shoe box to the bottom of one cardboard box. Set second box in front.
4. Put magazines in each cardboard box.

262

Theme Centers for Dramatic Play

Center Enhancements

Wall Map

Create or purchase a large map of your town. Display it on the wall or fence. Pinpoint points of interest (the school, gas station, car wash, library, train station).

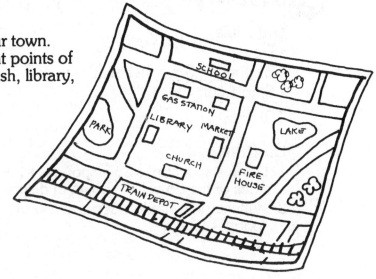

Food Posters

Display food promotion posters such as those found in quick-stop gas stations. Posters can also be created from magazine or newspaper ads and construction paper.

Drink Cup/Food-to-Go Bag

Decorate plain paper cups and brown paper bags with a gas station logo (suggestion: intertwining circles of varying sizes to suggest bubbles). Place containers at the serve-yourself food area.

PROPS TO MAKE

☼ SQUEEGEE

Materials
- Dowel
- 2 sponges, 3 x 5 inches (7.6 x 12.7 cm)
- Staple gun
- Stapler

Directions
1. Using staple gun, staple sponges to both sides of the dowel as shown in diagram.
2. With stapler, staple sides and top of sponges together.

☼ LICENSE PLATE FRAME

(Prop is appropriate for child participation)

Materials
- Tagboard
- Scissors
- License Plate Frame pattern (page 264)
- Magazines
- Glue

Directions
1. Duplicate pattern onto tagboard and cut out. Do not cut out center of frame.
2. Decorate with pictures, letters and numbers cut from magazines.

264

Theme Centers for Dramatic Play

Props to Make

☼ Windshield for Cars

Materials
- Cardboard
- Aluminum foil
- Duct tape
- Scissors

Directions
1. Cut pieces of cardboard to conform to the shape of bicycle handlebars. (Be sure they are low enough for children to see over.)
2. Cover cardboard with aluminum foil and secure with duct tape.
3. Attach "windshield" to handlebars of bicycle with duct tape.

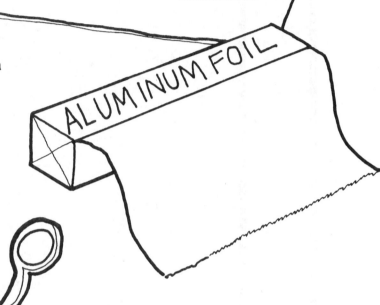

ALUMINUM FOIL

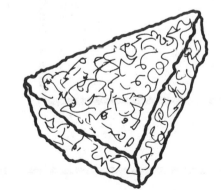

☼ Road Sign Shape Sponges

Materials
- Sponges
- Scissors

Directions
1. Cut sponges into basic road sign shapes.
2. Place in art center.

265

Prop Pattern

Theme Centers for Dramatic Play

CENTER TIPS

Introducing the Center
During circle time, ask open-ended questions about car, gas station, and car wash experiences. What happens at a gas station? Who can tell me something about a car wash? Encourage the children to add their own personal experiences and comments.

Safety Tips
- The "car" must drive carefully up to the gas pumps and through the car wash.
- The spray bottles are only used to clean the "cars."
- Only one "car" at a time may drive through the car wash.

CENTER VARIATIONS

Car rental office
- Add desk with phone, typewriter
- Add travel posters

267

Developmental Activities

Car Washing

Put out buckets of water, spray bottles and rags in the car wash to that children can wash the cars.

Skills To Build
- Acquiring skills with tools and equipment
- Large motor skills

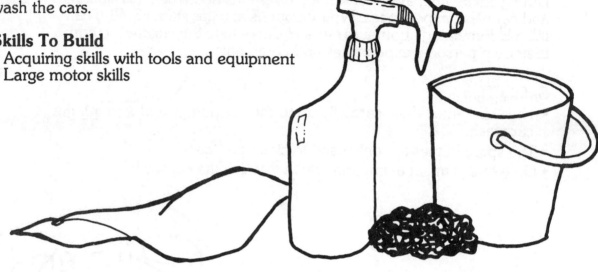

Sponge-Paint Road Sign Collage

Set out Road Sign Shape Sponges (Props to Make) and tempera paint, along with magazines, scissors, glue sticks and construction paper. Invite the children to create collages.

Skills To Build
- Small motor skills
- Drawing and painting

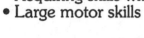

268

Theme Centers for Dramatic Play

Developmental Activities

☼ Fast-Food / Gas Purchase

Encourage the children to purchase food items, magazines, and gasoline at Bubble-Matic Gas Station. Join in the action to get the ball rolling.

Skills To Build
- Role-playing
- Imitating actions

☼ License Plate Frames

Allow children to design their own license plates with blank License Plate Frames (Props to Make), along with markers, glue and letters, words, and numbers cut from magazines.

Skills To Build
- Letter recognition
- Number recognition
- Spatial awareness
- Creative expression

Literature List

Picture Books

• **Cars**
by Angela Royston;
Macmillan 1991. (PS-2))
Double-page spreads introduce a
variety of cars.

• **Garage Song**
by Sarah Wilson;
Simon & Schuster 1991. (PS-K)
A young boy witnesses all the
activities that can be seen during a
day at a full-service garage.

• **Red Light Stop, Green Light Go**
by Andrew Kulman;
Simon & Schuster 1993. (PS-1)
A nonsense book about cars,
people, and animals—all waiting for
the green light.

• **An Auto Mechanic**
Dorling 1993. (K-3)
This occupation comes to life with
simple text and bright illustrations.

• **Cars**
Dorling 1993. (K-3)
By using a peeled-back diagram, the
exterior and interior of many autos
are shown.

• **My Lift-A-Flap Car Book**
by Angela Royston;
Putnam 1991. (PS-1)
A pop-up book that lets young
readers steer the car, turn the
wheels, and check under the hood.

Books to Read Aloud

• **Mr. Gumpy's Motor Car**
by John Burningham;
Harper LB 1976. (K-3)
Mr. Gumpy takes his daughter and
an assortment of animals for a ride
in the country in his touring car.

• **Jennifer and Josephine**
by Bill Peet;
Houghton 1980. (1-3)
Jennifer, an old touring car, is
driven through several adventures
by a reckless driver and a cat named
Josephine.

• **Little Auto**
by Lois Lenski;
McKay 1980. (K-3)
Adventures of the popular Mr.
Small.

• **Tin Lizzie**
by Peter Spier;
Doubleday 1990. (1-3)
The life and adventures of a single
Model-T Ford made in 1909.

• **Fill It Up! All About Service
Stations**
by Gail Gibbons;
Harper LB 1985. (K-3)
Children learn about the daily
activities of John & Peggy's service
station.

• **Mrs. Minetta's Car Pool**
by Elizabeth Spurr;
Macmillan 1985. (1-3)
Instead of driving the kids to school,
Mrs. Minetta takes them off on
glorious adventures.

270

RESOURCES & MORE ☺

☺ RESOURCES & RELATED ACTIVITIES

- Visit a gas station.

- Visit a car wash.

- Wash a car at school.

- Use a city map to locate car washes and gas stations in your area.

- Have a "bubble-fun" day and collect a variety of items to make bubbles.

- After "bubble-fun" day, make a chart of which items did or did not make good bubbles.

- In the parking lot at school, walk around and decide which cars are the dirtiest and need washing.

- Make a class chart of the types, colors, or numbers of cars each child's family has.

- Send a letter home to parents suggesting they take their child along to the drive-thru car wash. Later, share the experiences in class.

- Make a "car-wash" story book based on above experiences. Have each child dictate and then draw a picture.

- Make a list of the foods you find at a gas station. Discuss whether they are "good-healthy" foods.

- Put out ingredients to make a beverage from a mix or concentrate in the food store. (Hint: provide a drop cloth under the preparation area.)

271

Dear Parents:

We are preparing a Bubble-Matic Car Wash Theme Center in our classroom during these dates: _____. This center will provide an opportunity for the children to participate in dramatic play and will serve as a basis for classroom discussion and learning activities. Below you will find a list of items that we need to furnish the center:

☐ Sponges & rags   ☐ Rubber shoes

☐ Beverage to make   ☐ Coveralls

☐ Duct tape   ☐ Spray bottle

☐ Aluminum foil   ☐ Whisk broom

☐ Roadmaps   ☐ _____

Please return items checked by _____.

You can support the use of this center by talking to your child about the theme, planning family excursions related to the theme, or by sharing books that will provide your child with more information. A suggested literature list is available upon request.

Parent Name _____

Phone Number _____ ☐ I would love to help!

© Edupress   *Theme Centers for Dramatic Play*

Kid's Gym

KID GYM

KID GYM

Center Set-Up

🙂 Floorplan

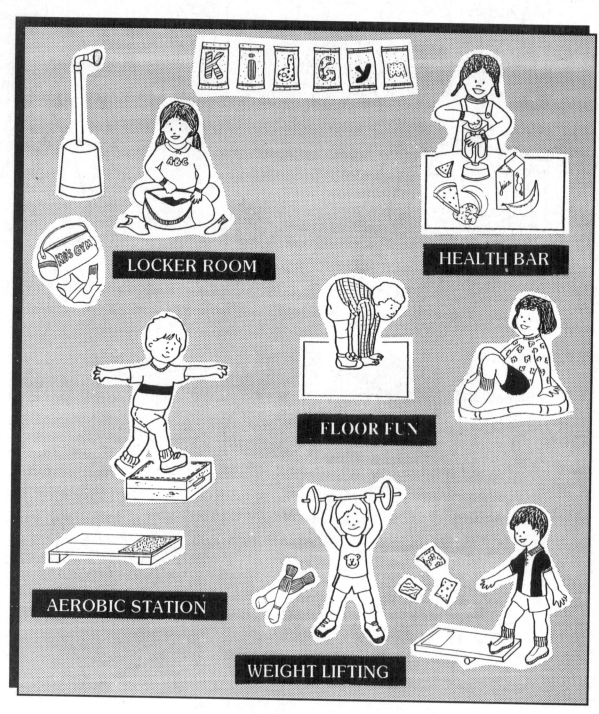

KiD GyM

LOCKER ROOM

HEALTH BAR

FLOOR FUN

AEROBIC STATION

WEIGHT LIFTING

274

Theme Centers for Dramatic Play

CENTER SET-UP

☼ FURNISHINGS AND ACCESSORIES

Weight Lifting
- Barbells (Props to Make)
- Free Weights (Props to Make)
- Beanbags
- Launcher (Props to Make)

Health Bar
- Bowls
- Stools
- Cups, plates
- Play fruits & vegetables
- Blender (Props to Make)
- Empty yogurt containers
- Picture books of fruits & vegetables

Gym Bag
- Shorts
- Tank tops
- Leotards
- Sweatbands
- T-shirts
- Tights
- Socks
- Gloves
- Sweat pants
- Sweatshirts

Floor Fun
- Record or tape player
- Mats
- Floor-length mirror
- VCR & exercise tapes (Resources)

Aerobic Station
- Treadmill (Bare-Budget Furnishings)
- Step (Bare-Budget Furnishings)
- Stationary bicycle

Locker Room
- Shower (Center Enhancements)
- Scale
- Additional gym bags of various sizes
- Towels

275

Theme Centers for Dramatic Play

Bare-Budget Furnishings

Treadmill

Materials

- Two 12-inch x 36-inch (30.4 cm x 1 m) pre-cut shelves
- Two wooden 2 x 4s
- Hammer
- Nails
- Vinyl contact paper **or** carpet remnants

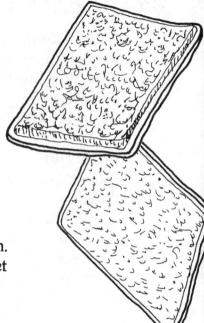

Directions

1. Lay the shelves across the 2 x 4 supports, as shown.
2. Nail the shelves to the supports, leaving no gap between.
3. Cover the surface with vinyl contact paper or with carpet remnants held in place with staples from a staple gun.

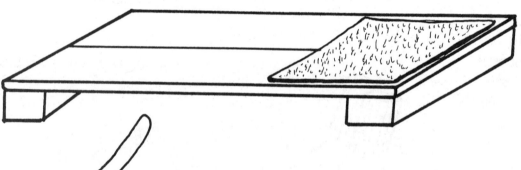

Step Exerciser

Use a staple gun to cover a low wooden or plastic crate* with a vinyl place mat cut to fit.

* Check with you local food store.

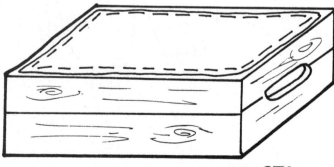

CENTER ENHANCEMENTS

Shower

Invert a large plastic plant container. Insert a PVC pipe fitted with a threaded PVC elbow and plastic garden hose spray attachment.

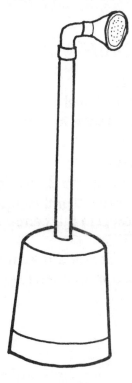

Gym Bags

Store dramatic play clothing and other center props in duffel or gym bags marked KIDS GYM.

Wall Sign

Recycle old towels to create a colorful wall sign announcing the name of the center. Cut manuscript letters from cloth or paper to attach to towels. Mount on wall.

Props to Make

Barbell

Materials
- Wooden dowel
- 2 Styrofoam™ circles

Directions
1. Cut dowel into 2-foot (61 cm) lengths.
2. Cut a circle slightly larger than the diameter of the dowel in the center of each Styrofoam™ circle.
3. Slide a Styrofoam™ circle over each end of the dowel approximately 4 inches (10 cm) from the end.

Free Weights

Materials
- Tube sports sock
- Fiberfill™ stuffing
- Dried beans
- Sewing machine (**or needle and thread**)
- 2 rubber bands

Directions
1. Lightly stuff the sock with Fiberfill™. Add a few beans for weight.
2. Sew the open end of sock closed.
3. Wrap a rubber band about 2 inches (5 cm) from each sock end.

278

Theme Centers for Dramatic Play

PROPS TO MAKE

BLENDER

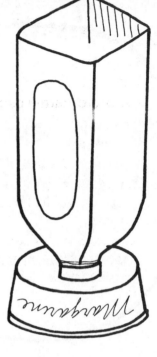

Materials
- Plastic milk container
- Margarine tub
- Masking tape

Directions
1. Cut the bottom off the clean milk container.
2. Cut an opening in the tub lid the approximated diameter of the milk container mouth.
3. Insert the inverted milk container and push the mouth into the hole in the lid. Tape in place.

LAUNCHER

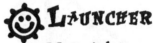

Materials
- 6 x 18-inch (15 x 45.7 cm) piece of plywood
- 5½-inch (14 cm) length of 1-inch (2.54 cm) dowel
- Paint   • Marker

Directions
1. Sand plywood until smooth.
2. File two sides of dowel until flat.
3. Nail one flat side across the width of the plywood, about 5 inches (12.5 cm) from one end.
4. Paint the board a bright color.
5. Draw a square on the top of the board, opposite the dowel end. Draw stars on the top of the other end of the board.

FITNESS FRUIT

Reproduce fruit patterns (following page) on white or colored construction paper for use in the Health Bar.

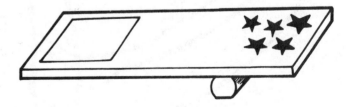

Theme Centers for Dramatic Play

280

Theme Centers for Dramatic Play

☺ CENTER TIPS

Introducing the Center
Teach some simple stretching activities during circle time. Watch an exercise video (see Resources) and complete the exercises together.

Safety Tips
• Demonstrate the use of all center equipment, including running in place on the treadmill and riding the stationary tricycle.
• Determine the number of children who will be in the center at one time.
• Explain that children will need to allow lots of space around them when using the weights and launcher. Role-play this situation.

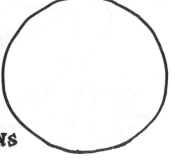

☺ CENTER VARIATIONS

Relaxation Center
Clear everything out of the center and cover the floor area with mats. Play soft music and place picture books and pillows in the area.

Health and Fitness Store
Remove the exercise equipment and replace it with shelves and tables stocked with empty vitamin containers, play fruits and vegetables, and empty bags for shopping.

Coordination Center
Promote coordination skills by removing large motor "exercise" equipment and adding things that develop small motor skills, such as tennis shoes to lace, foam balls to toss and catch, and assorted bags and backpacks to zip, buckle, and snap.

☀ DEVELOPMENTAL ACTIVITIES

☀ PACK A GYM BAG

Get ready for a workout by packing a duffel bag with exercise clothes.

Skills To Build
• Spatial awareness
• Size comparison
• Small motor

☀ FRUIT FUN

Use the fruit patterns (page 280) to create collages or "blend" fruit drinks at the Health Bar.

Skills To Build
• Small motor
• Object identification
• Object association

278

Developmental Activities

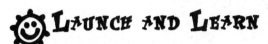

☺ Launch and Learn

Develop coordination with fun-filled launchers.
Follow the step-by-step instructions.

1. Place bean bag on square.
2. Step on opposite end of launcher.
3. Catch bean bag.

Skills To Build
• Eye-hand coordination
• Spatial awareness

☺ Muscle Magic

"Build" muscles with weight-lifting activities.

Skills To Build
• Body awareness

LITERATURE LIST

PICTURE BOOKS

• **Your Insides**
by Joanna Cole;
Putnam 1992. (PS-1)
Clear overlays help to explain the
workings of the human body for the
young reader.

• **Wiggle-Butts and Up-Faces**
by Irene M. Kolbison;
I Think I Can 1989. (PS-K)
Ingrid's young brother is afraid of
taking beginner swimming lessons.

• **The Bear's Bicycle**
by Emilie W. McLeod;
Little paper 1986. (PS-2)
A small boy and his teddy bear have
an exciting bicycle ride as he gives
the bear safety lessons.

• **The Adventures of Albert, the
Running Bear**
by Barbara Isenberg & Susan Wolf;
Houghton 1982 (PS-2)
Albert, a chubby bear, accidentally
wins the Annual City Marathon.

• **My Body**
by Angela Royston;
Dorling 1991. (PS-2)
A basic introduction to anatomy,
using photos and drawings.

• **Albie the Lifeguard**
by Louise Borden;
Scholastic 1993. (PS-3)
Albie is not a confident swimmer,
but in his backyard he fantasizes
about being a lifeguard.

BOOKS TO READ ALOUD

• **The Big Mile Race**
by Leonard Kessler;
Dell paper 1991. (1-3)
A group of animals engage in a
marathon.

• **Home Field**
by David Spohn;
Lothrop LB 1993. (PS-2)
When Matt and his dad go out to
play a simple game of baseball, the
boy feels he is in a sports stadium.

• **Charles T. McBiddle**
by Andrew Glass;
Bantam 1993. (K-2)
A beast taunts Charles with every
failure in his attempts to ride a
regular bicycle.

• **Sugargrandpa**
by David M. Schwartz;
Lothrop LB 1992. (1-3)
This story of a grandfather who won
the longest bike race in Sweden is
based on fact.

• **I'm Growing!**
by Aliki;
Harper LB 1992. (PS-1)
Basic concepts of physiology are
explained in this simple story of a
young boy who is delighted to grow
bigger.

• **Old Turtle's Soccer Team**
by Leonard Kessler;
Greenwillow LB 1985. (1-2)
Old Turtle's team gets in shape to
face the Big Raccoon's Rockets

284

RESOURCES & MORE

RESOURCES & RELATED ACTIVITIES

- Exercise videos suitable for children.

- Invite a fitness trainer to teach children some simple exercises.

- Ask a weight-lifter to demonstrate his or her skill. Point out muscles in the body.

- Visit a local gym or fitness center to watch exercise in action.

- Make some simple fitness comparisons:
  - Run in place and compare your breathing before and after.
  - Compare the difference between lifting heavy and light objects.
  - Practice flexing your muscles and feeling the difference in the body.

- Learn some simple exercises to do in the "gym."
  - toe-touching
  - stretching
  - running in place
  - jumping jacks

- Introduce children to healthy eating and teach some basic skills at the same time.
  - Blend fruit and juice to make smoothies for snack. Observe the changes in the fruit from solid to smooth.

  - Develop small motor skills by peeling and slicing or sectioning bananas or oranges.

  - Count the grapes on a bunch as they are passed out for a tasty treat.

Theme Centers for Dramatic Play

Dear Parents:

We are preparing a Kid's Gym Theme Center in our classroom during these dates: _____. This center will provide an opportunity for the children to participate in dramatic play and will serve as a basis for classroom discussion and learning activities. Below you will find a list of items that we need to furnish the center:

☐ Wooden dowel   ☐ 12 x 36-inch shelf

☐ Margarine tub   ☐ Plastic milk carton

☐ Bean bag   ☐ Duffel bag

☐ Tube sport sock   ☐ Gym bag

☐ Clean towel   ☐ _____

Please return the items checked by _____.

You can support the use of this center by talking to your child about the theme, planning family excursions related to the theme, or by sharing books that will provide your child with more information. A suggested literature list is available upon request.

Parent Name _____

Phone Number _____ ☐ I would love to help!

© Edupress   *Theme Centers for Dramatic Play*

☼ FLOORPLAN

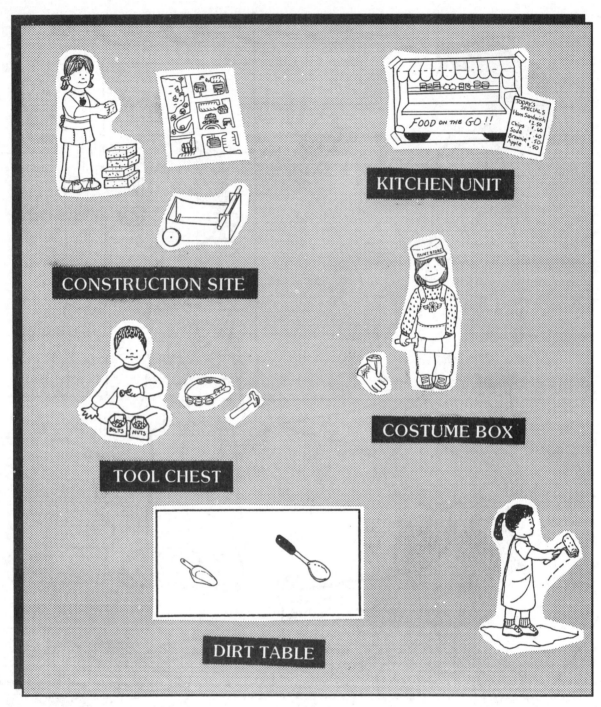

KITCHEN UNIT

CONSTRUCTION SITE

COSTUME BOX

TOOL CHEST

DIRT TABLE

Center Set-Up

☼ Furnishings and Accessories

Construction Site
- Wheelbarrow (Bare-Budget Furnishings)
- Road Rug (Bare-Budget Furnishings)
- Bricks (Props to Make)
- Toy construction materials

Water Table
- Brushes
- Paint rollers
- Shaving cream
- Plaster trowels
- Putty knives
- Sieves & strainers
- Empty cans
- Sponges

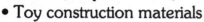

Costume Box
- Denim shorts
- Jeans
- Boots
- Work socks
- Work gloves
- Hard Hat (Props to Make)
- Painters hats
- Coveralls

Dirt Table
- (change to sand or sawdust)
- Scoops
- Small hand shovels
- Measuring cups & spoons

Kitchen Unit
- Coffee cups & coffee pot
- Plastic food (wrapped)—sandwiches, fruit, donuts, bagels, burritos, chips

Art Center
- Nuts, bolts, screws, washers, nails
- Juice can lids
- Tacky glue
- Margarine tubs or small plastic bins

Tool Chest
- Hammers
- Nail Apron (Props to Make)
- Saws (To be used with teacher direction)
- Tool Belt (Props to Make)
- Screwdrivers
- Measuring Tape (Props to Make)

Center Set-Up

Bare-Budget Furnishings

Wheelbarrow
Materials
- Cardboard box, 2 x 3 x 2 feet (61 x 91 x 61 cm)
- Dowel, ½ x 28 inches (1.17 x 71 cm)
- Dowel, ½ x 36 inches (1.17 cm x 1 m)
- Exacto® knife   • 2 nails
- Cardboard   • Hammer
- Glue

Directions
1. Cut cardboard box with Exacto® knife as shown in diagram.
2. Cut holes in box as shown in diagram.
3. Slide dowels through holes, the shorter one in the lower front holes.
4. Cut six 6-inch (15 cm) circles from cardboard.
5. Glue two sets of three circles together.
6. Nail circles to ends of shorter dowel for wheels.

Road Rug
Materials
- White sheet
- Fabric markers or tempera paint.

Directions
1. Before you mark the sheet, draw a scale model on a sheet of paper.
2. Draw roads and buildings on the sheet. Suggestions: school, post office, hospital, fire department, police station, park, airport, houses, marina, church.

CENTER ENHANCEMENTS

Building Frame

Use paint, markers or crayons to create a building frame on butcher paper to use as a backdrop on a wall or fence.

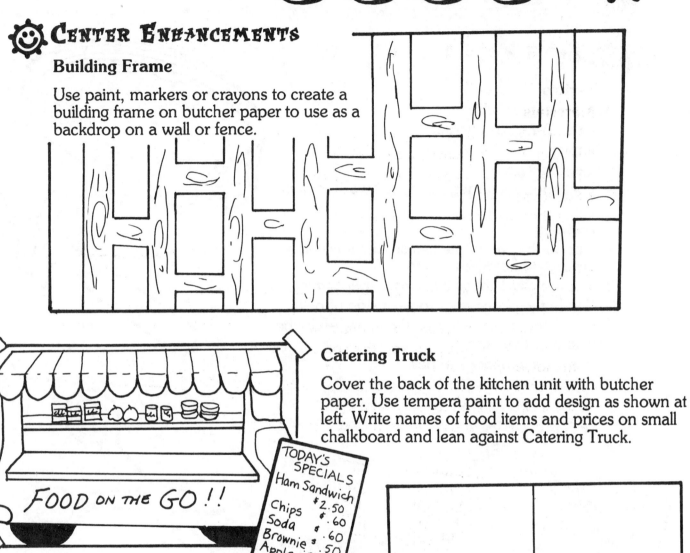

FOOD ON THE GO !!

TODAY'S SPECIALS
Ham Sandwich $2.50
Chips $ .60
Soda $ .60
Brownie $ .50
Apple $ .50

Catering Truck

Cover the back of the kitchen unit with butcher paper. Use tempera paint to add design as shown at left. Write names of food items and prices on small chalkboard and lean against Catering Truck.

Painting Wall

Use a large cardboard box cut open at one seam. Unfold and duct tape bottom to the ground. Place plastic drop cloth around the base. Provide trays of paint (water soluble) and rollers and brushes.

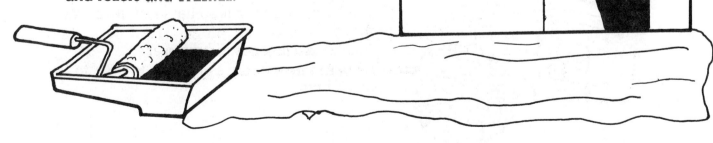

Props to Make

☺ Tool Belt

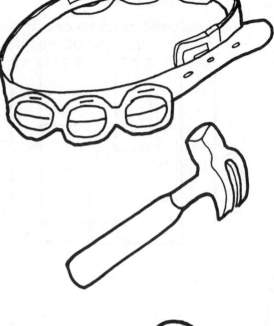

Materials
- Small leather belt
- Plastic 6-ring can holder
- Stapler
- Masking tape
- Small tools (hammer, pliers, screwdriver, tape)

Directions
1. Cut off the end of the belt so that it will fit a child. Add holes, if needed.
2. Cut the plastic rings into two, 3-ring strips.
3. Staple the plastic rings to each side of belt.
4. Cover the staple points on the inside of the belt with masking tape.
3. Put tools into loops of belt.

☺ Hard Hat

Materials
- 8-inch (20 cm) diameter plastic bowl
- Coffee can lid   • Hole punch
- Yarn   • Scissors
- Tape

Directions
1. Cut the brim for the hard hat from the coffee can lid.
2. Punch holes in ends of brim piece.
3. Tie yarn through loops and tape to bowl to attach brim.

292

PROPS TO MAKE

NAIL APRON

Materials
- White dish towel
- Yarn
- Needle & thread

Directions
1. Fold dish towel over 1 inch (2.54 cm) on long side. Stitch casing.
2. Fold up the bottom third of dish towel. Stitch sides.
3. Stitch to form pockets as shown.
4. Slip yarn through casing.

MEASURING TAPE

Materials
- Toilet paper tube
- 1 yard (1 m) single-fold bias tape
- Stapler
- Marker

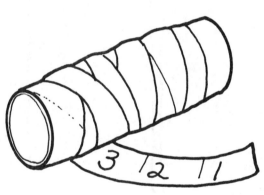

Directions
1. Mark lines at 1-inch (2.54 cm) intervals on bias tape and number.
2. Staple tape to toilet paper tube at 36-inch (1 m) mark and wind up.

BRICKS

Materials for One
- Brick pattern, following page
- Food box
- White paper
- Tacky glue
- Crayons

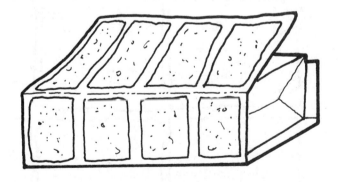

Directions
1. Photocopy brick pattern onto white paper.
1. Color bricks.
2. Cover box with paper using tacky glue.

Prop Pattern

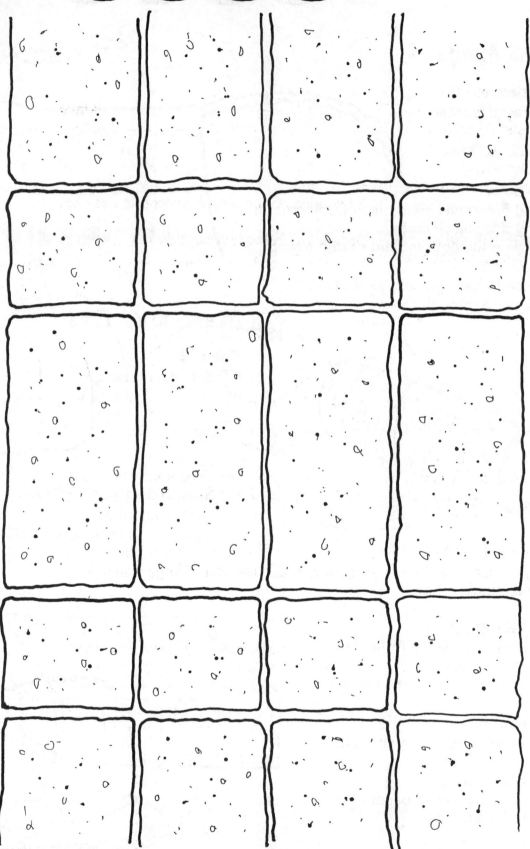

294

Theme Centers for Dramatic Play

TEACHING TIPS

☀ CENTER TIPS

Introducing the Center
During circle time read Eric Carle's *The Apron*. Talk about what it take to build a house. Ask children what they know about building a house.

Safety Tips
• Children must be instructed in how and where to use tools. The individual teacher is the best judge about what is appropriate for her children.
• Start with the centers (wood, paint) being teacher-directed, and then have more child-directed as time passes.

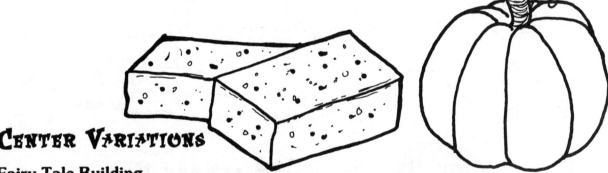

☀ CENTER VARIATIONS

Fairy Tale Building
Provide sticks, straw, bricks for *The Three Little Pigs* houses. Set out old shoes for *The Old Woman Who Lived in a Shoe* and a pumpkin for *Peter, Peter, Pumpkin Eater*.

Houses in Other Lands
Set out ice cubes in water table to make igloos and large leaves to make jungle houses.

Animal Houses
Provide twigs for bird's nests, cotton balls, yarn and fabric for bunny nests, and gravel and small stones for reptile houses.

Theme Centers for Dramatic Play

DEVELOPMENTAL ACTIVITIES

PAINT THE WALL

Put out paint trays, cans of paint (water soluble), brushes, and rollers. Let children paint the wall.

Skills To Build
- Large muscle skills
- Discover through direct experience
- Acquiring skills with tools

ASSEMBLE NUTS 'N BOLTS 'N WASHERS

Set out an assortment of nuts, bolts and washers in bins. Invite the children to assemble and disassemble them.

Skills To Build
- Fine motor skills
- Pincer grip—become ready to write
- Manipulating and combining objects
- Sorting
- Identifying similarities and differences

Developmental Activities

☼ Nut and Bolt Sculpture

Use the metal tops of frozen juice cans, nuts, bolts, washers and tacky glue to create a sculpture.

Skills To Build
• Observing and placing objects from different points of view
• Creating with unusual materials

☼ Build with Bricks

Invite children to build structures with bricks.

Skills To Build
• Exploring the way things go together
• Making model out of blocks

297

LITERATURE LIST

PICTURE BOOKS

• **My First Look at Home**
Random 1991. (PS)
The concept of a home is
introduced with color photos.

• **Tools**
by Venice Shone;
Scholastic 1991. (PS-K)
Simple tools used in such activities
as woodworking, gardening, and
painting are pictured and identified.

• **How a House Is Built**
by Gail Gibbons;
Holiday 1990. (PS-K)
A good introduction to the
construction of a wood frame
house.

• **Girders and Cranes: A
Skyscraper Is Built**
by Lee Balterman;
Whitman 1991 (PS-3)
Describes the building of a 67-story
skyscraper in Chicago.

• **Harry Builds a House**
by Derek Radford;
Macmillan 1990. (PS-1)
Every step of the construction of the
house built by Harry Hippo and his
friends is pictured.

• **Houses**
by Katharine Carter;
Childrens LB 1982. (K-3)
Types of houses and how they are
constructed.

BOOKS TO READ ALOUD

• **This Is My House**
by Arthur Dorros;
Scholastic 1992. (K-2)
Various houses from around the
world that represent different
peoples are pictured and identified.

• **This Is A House**
by Colleen S. Bare;
Dutton 1992. (1-3)
A step-by-step description of how a
house is built.

• **From Blueprint to House**
by Franz Hogner;
Carolrhoda 1986. (K-3)
Working from an architects plan, a
building is constructed.

• **The Toolbox**
by Anne Rockwell
Macmillan 1971. (1-2)
A description of each tool in the
toolbox and what it does.

• **Victoria House**
by Janice Shefelman;
Harcourt 1988. (PS-2)
Sarah, an architect, sees beyond the
disrepair of Victoria House and
restores its beauty.

• **New House**
by Joyce Maynard;
Harcourt 1987. (PS-1)
Explaining in story form how a
house is built.

Theme Centers for Dramatic Play

RESOURCES & MORE

☺ RESOURCES & RELATED ACTIVITIES

- Go to a building site and watch the process from a safe distance.

- Visit a hardware store.

- Buy nails, screws, nuts, bolts, washers at a hardware store.

- Visit a saw mill (if there is one locally).

- Visit a paint store.

- Invite a carpenter to visit and share the contents of his or her toolbox.

- Invite a parent who is a painter to visit.

- Have parent helpers come and teach the children to hammer, saw and paint.

- As a class, make a small structure such as a chair or table or fence by hammering.

- Make a mural on butcher paper by painting with a variety of brushes and rollers.

- Use real measuring tapes to measure things around school.

- Put out a variety of nuts, bolts, screws in one bin—set out other empty bins for sorting.

- Explore the concepts of before and after by completing these simple construction projects:
    - Nail two small pieces of wood together.
    - Paint a piece of wood a bright color.
    - Hammer a nail until it is bent.

- Develop tactile skills by hand-sanding a rough surface.

Theme Centers for Dramatic Play

Dear Parents:

We are preparing a Top Floor Construction Theme Center in our classroom during these dates: _____. This center will provide an opportunity for the children to participate in dramatic play and will serve as a basis for classroom discussion and learning activities. Below you will find a list of items that we need to furnish the center:

☐ Paint   ☐ Nuts, bolts, screws, washers or nails

☐ Hammers   ☐ Milk carton

☐ Screwdriver   ☐ Shoe box

☐ Saw   ☐ Dish towel

☐ Wood   ☐ _____

Please return the items checked below by _____.

You can support the use of this center by talking to your child about the theme, planning family excursions related to the theme, or by sharing books that will provide your child with more information. A suggested literature list is available upon request.

Parent Name _____

Phone Number _____ ☐ I would love to help!

300

PROPS & FURNISHINGS

ABOUT DRAMATIC PLAY

Dramatic play centers provide a wealth of opportunities for children to exercise their imaginations and build a variety of important cognitive and social skills. Dramatic play allows social interaction with fellow students in a friendly setting. Role imitation provides insight into the real world while still engaging in the world of "pretend." Dramatic play centers provide a safe environment for exploration and growth. They can also serve as the basis for developing anti-bias behavior.

TEACHING TIPS

- **General guidelines.** Items in disrepair (unless it's a Fix-it Center) are not generally successful. Providing too much of anything is confusing to children and does not allow the opportunity for learning to share. Establish center procedures with which the children become familiar. These routines can be sustained from day to day and center to center. Constantly make connections between school, home, and community. Involve children in suggesting ideas and adding to each center. These connections are invaluable in developing critical thinking skills.

- **Teacher intervention.** Enter the dramatic play space as you "pass by," only to become an extension of the role-playing. Some children may need you as a role model in "how to play." After one center has been introduced, the children will feel more comfortable in the setting and will no longer need guidance in how to participate in the center activities.

  Instruction is not a part of the center because the activities are developmentally-based. Direct intervention *may* take place to introduce a prop. This can be achieved during circle time or outside the center, as well. Children will watch and learn from their classmates. Obviously, if unsafe actions are observed, intervention is necessary.

- **Time Management.** Some general guidelines to follow are: Student play peaks at 20 minutes although 40 minutes is recommended two or three times per week. Allow free movement in and out of the center. Carefully monitor the number of children in the center at one time. Intervene to move children out if the center becomes too crowded for safe play. Children will usually interact in pairs although individual play is also constructive.

- **Center Variation.** Be sure to include some of the centers that are set up outdoors. This will allow some freedom of movement in and out of the center space and enhance awareness. Carefully observe the changing interest level in the center. Add variations or change props to keep interest at a constructive level.

- **Observing and evaluating.** Take time to observe each child as he or she participates in the center. Look for important social skills. Make note of motor development. Observe creativity. Take time to complete an observation log (following page) for each child. This observation log can serve as a valuable tool when evaluating student growth, setting goals, and conferences with parents. Date the observation log and complete a new one later in the year to chart skill growth and compare the differences in skill development, imaginative play, and social interaction.

302

© Edupress   *Theme Centers for Dramatic Play*

OBSERVATION LOG

Name_____ Age_____

Social Interaction_____

Development_____

Creativity_____

Decision Making_____

Additional Comments_____